Deluxe
Ninja Dual Zone
Air Fryer Cookbook

2000+ Days Quick and Easy Healthy Recipes with Tips & Tricks|Approved by Thousands of Beginners|UK Measurements [2024 FULL COLOUR EDITION]

Lauren Leonard

© Copyright 2024 –All Rights Reserved

This document is geared towards providing exact and reliable information concerning the topic and issue covered.

In no way is it legal to reproduce, duplicate, or transmit any part of this document in either electronic means or printed format. Recording this publication is strictly prohibited. Any storage of this document is not allowed unless with written permission from the publisher.

All rights reserved. The information provided herein is stated to be truthful and consistent, in that any liability, in terms of inattention or otherwise, by any usage or abuse of any policies, processes, or directions contained within is the solitary and utter responsibility of the recipient reader.

Under no circumstances will any legal responsibility or blame be held against the publisher for any reparation, damages, or monetary loss due to the information herein, either directly or indirectly. Respective authors own all copyrights not held by the publisher.

The information herein is offered for informational purposes solely and is universal as so. The presentation of the information is without a contract or any type of guarantee assurance. The trademarks used are without any consent, and the publication of any trademark is without permission or backing by the trademark owner.

All trademarks and brands within this book are for clarifying purposes only, are owned by the owners themselves, and are not affiliated with this document.

Table of Contents

- 1 Introduction
- 2 Fundamentals of Ninja Foodi Dual Zone Air Fryer
- 16 4-Week Meal Plan
- 18 Chapter 1 Breakfast
- 26 Chapter 2 Vegetables and Sides
- 32 Chapter 3 Poultry
- 38 Chapter 4 Beef, Pork, and Lamb
- 45 Chapter 5 Fish and Seafood
- 50 Chapter 6 Snacks and Starters
- 57 Chapter 7 Desserts
- 65 Conclusion
- 66 Appendix 1 Measurement Conversion Chart
- 67 Appendix 2 Air Fryer Cooking Chart
- 68 Appendix 3 Recipes Index

Introduction

Because of the busy day and tight schedules many people experience, cooking different meals has become quite tough. However, with the Ninja Foodi Dual Zone Air Fryer, you will have everything in perfect order.

There are other air fryer versions, but the Ninja Foodi Dual one is exceptional because of its unique features. You will love the dual basket feature, an option that makes it possible to make different meals on the go, thanks to the dual functionality.

What's more, you will get delicious and nutritious meals with a perfect finish when you use the Ninja Foodi Dual Zone Air Fryer for cooking. Ideally, you will never have to visit any nearby food outlet or restaurant for that perfect snack you've always admired. The Ninja Foodi Dual Zone Air Fryer has got you covered.

For all your parties and gatherings, you can use the Ninja Foodi Dual Zone Air Fryer to prepare more food. Whether you want to bake, dehydrate, reheat, roast, air fry, or want crispy food, the Ninja Foodi Dual Zone Air Fryer has all these functionalities.

Make cakes, pancakes, and muffins of varied flavors for your breakfast ideas. Roast or fry fish, chicken, veggies, and any other meal for snacking, lunch, or even dinner. Even if you are just starting, you won't have a hard time using this great appliance.

This guide has lots of recipes you can begin with once you read the details of how to get the most out of your Ninja Foodi Dual Zone Air Fryer.

Fundamentals of Ninja Foodi Dual Zone Air Fryer

What is the Ninja Foodi Dual Zone Air Fryer?

The Ninja Foodi Dual Zone Air Fryer is a simple-to-use, sophisticated, and modern kitchen appliance used to cook healthy meals quite quickly compared to other cooking appliances. Unlike the basic air fryer, the Ninja Foodi Dual Zone Air Fryer comes with 2 baskets for cooking more food at a go, hence the name dual air fryer.

You can make healthy, flavorful, and colorful meals in the comfort of your home, thanks to the amazing Ninja Foodi Dual Zone Air Fryer. When compared with other traditional frying methods, you will use less oil when you use the Ninja Foodi Dual Zone Air Fryer.

The appliance comes fitted with a nonstick cooking basket that is easy to detach from the appliance without messing the working surface with grease or oil spillages. The interior and exterior part of the Ninja Foodi Dual Zone Air Fryer is made with solid stainless-steel materials, giving it a sleek appearance and making it durable. One safety feature of this kitchen appliance is the automatic shut-off feature that enables the equipment to shut off when it reaches the set temperature or when it runs out of power.

Since the appliance is made with stainless steel materials, it is easy to clean & maintain. What's more, the two air fryer baskets make it simple to cook more food on the go. You can cook meals to serve together or use on different occasions. It all depends on your meal plans, what you need at a particular time, and the people you are serving. The baskets come with a tight lid, ensuring they hold the food in position throughout the cooking time. This makes the device even more convenient.

The Dual Zone Technology

This dual air fryer equipment uses dual technology, whereby you can cook the meals through two zones. Even though the cooking requirements for the meals you are preparing might be different, the appliance has a sync feature, making sure that all the meals finish cooking at the same time.

Smart Finish

How to use the SMART FINISH feature on the Ninja Foodi Dual Zone Air Fryer to cook (different functions, different times, and different temperatures)?

To activate the sync feature, follow the steps below in case the meals have different temperatures and cooking times and require different cooking functions:

- Add the ingredients into the drawers before setting them into the Ninja Foodi Dual Zone Air Fryer.
- For zone 1, select the appropriate cooking functionality once it is lit, then set the temperature with the "TEMP" arrows and the time with the "TIME" arrows.
- For zone 2, select the appropriate cooking functionality, then use the "TEMP" arrows to set the temperature and the "TIME" arrows to set the time.
- Click the SMART FINISH, then the START/PAUSE function to begin the process on the zone with the longest cooking time. You will see Hold on the opposite zone. When the same left to cook all the meals is the same, the Ninja Foodi Dual Zone Air Fryer will automatically beep and activate the other zone to start the cooking process.
- Once the cooking time is over, you will see "END" on the display, showing the food is ready.
- Remove the meals using tongs or any other appropriate kitchen equipment. Avoid putting the drawer over the Ninja Foodi Dual Zone Air Fryer.

Match Cook

How to use the MATCH COOK feature on the Ninja Foodi Dual Zone Air Fryer to prepare more quantity of the same food (same function, same temperature, and same time)?

- Add all ingredients to the drawers before putting them in place.
- Zone 1 will lot up. Select the appropriate cooking functionality, then set the temperature with the TEMP arrows and the time with the TIME arrows.
- Select MATCH COOK to extend the Zone 1 setting to Zone 2, then press the START/PAUSE functionality to start the cooking process on Zone 1 and zone 2.
- Once the food is fully cooked, you will see "END" on both screens.
- Remove the cooked meals carefully with the appropriate kitchen equipment.

Then how to begin the cooking process at the same time but finishing at different times?
- Select zone 1, then click on the appropriate cooking function.
- Next, set the temperatures with the TEMP arrows and the time with the TIME arrows.
- Do the exact processes for zone 2, then select the START/PAUSE function to start the cooking process.
- Stop the zone in which the food has already been cooked, even if the set timer isn't over yet. Select that zone, then press START/PAUSE to pause the zone or set the time to zero.
- You will hear a beep, then see the "end" on the display when the cooking time is over on both zones.
- Remove the ingredients appropriately and serve.

Basic Functional Buttons of the Ninja Foodi Dual Zone Air Fryer

Below are the basic functions of a Ninja Foodi Dual Zone Air Fryer you should know:

Temperature arrows:
It is used to set the temperatures based on the meal you are making or according to the guidelines on the recipe. Use the up and down arrows to adjust the cook temperature before or during cooking.

Time arrows:
It is used to adjust the cooking time as per the instructions on the recipe. Use the up and down arrows to

adjust the cook time in any function before or during the cook cycle.

Smart Finish button:
It is used to automatically syncs the cook times to ensure both zones finish at the same time, even if there are different cook times.

Match Cook button:
It is used to automatically matches zone 2 settings to those of zone 1 to cook a larger amount of the same food, or cook different foods using the same function, temperature, and time.

Start/Pause button:
This is a button you press to initiate a function. It can be cooking, resuming cooking, or initiating the cooking process. To pause cooking, first select the zone you would like to pause, then press the START/PAUSE button.

Power button:
You press the power button to switch on the appliance and when you need to turn it off. Also, you can use this button to stop all cooking functions.

Hold mode:
Hold will appear on the unit while in SMART FINISH mode. One zone will be cooking, while the other zone will be holding until the times sync together.

Benefits of a Ninja Foodi Dual Zone Air Fryer

If you are still contemplating whether to buy the Ninja Foodi Dual Zone Air Fryer or not, below are some of the reasons why this appliance will come in handy.

Convenience
Ideally, cooking requires more time investment, and it can be tiring at some time. This is the reason why most people will opt to buy ready-made meals. However, with the Ninja Foodi Dual Zone Air Fryer, the cooking process is more convenient. You can leave the meals to cook as you attend to other tasks, as long as you set the required functionalities.

Spacious
Unlike the traditional air fryer, the Ninja Foodi Dual Zone Air Fryer has two drawers, with each drawer having enough space to cook more food at a go. If you have a bigger family, this will always come in handy.

Sync Function

Since the Ninja Foodi Dual Zone Air Fryer comes with two zones, it is easy to program it according to your preference, thanks to the sync functionality. This means you can cook meals that require different cooking times to finish at the same time.

Faster than traditional ovens
You won't spend hours in the kitchen making food when using the Ninja Foodi Dual Zone Air Fryer.

It is safe
Ideally, in traditional deep fryers, it is easy for hot oil to splash, thus causing burns. Besides, what if you slide in the kitchen when the traditional deep fryer is on with hot oil? You are likely to get serious injuries. With the Ninja Foodi Dual Zone Air Fryer, you have maximum safety because the appliance doesn't need a lot of oil, prevents hot oil from splattering and avoiding burns. At the same time, you get a perfectly cooked meal.

Healthy
Since the Ninja Foodi Dual Zone Air Fryer doesn't require plenty, and sometimes no oil, it enhances the production of healthy meals for healthy living.

Easy to use
Even if you are a beginner, you won't have a hard time using the Ninja Foodi Dual Zone Air Fryer. It has clear functions that will direct you, apart from the detailed manual.

Highly versatile
The Ninja Foodi Dual Zone Air Fryer can perform different cooking requirements on the go. Whether it's baking, roasting, air frying, air broiling, reheating, or dehydrating, the appliance will definitely handle all this for you.

Saves money and kitchen space
Once you acquire the Ninja Foodi Dual Zone Air Fryer, you will realize you don't need other kitchen appliances for preparing different meals. This is because the equipment performs more functions and takes up less space in the kitchen, thus saving you time and money!

Before First Use

Once you purchase and unbox the unit, make sure you do the cleaning first as you inspect any possible damages. This will ensure your safety measures are in place and that your device is fully functional. In any case, always clean the appliance after every use to leave it in a good state that will guarantee a long life.
For cleaning, follow the steps highlighted below:
- Unplug the Ninja Foodi Dual Zone Air Fryer from the socket, then wait until it cools completely.
- Remove the other parts and accessories, put them in a dishwasher, or you can opt to hand clean them.
- Clean them using soapy water.
- For stubborn and tough stains on the baskets and crisper plates, soak them in warm and soapy water for a few minutes before the actual cleaning.
- Use a damp cloth that is clean to wipe the main unit.
- Once you clean everything, dry it thoroughly before assembling it back into the unit.

For maintenance, always check your equipment regularly for any possible damages.

Different Cooking Functions of the Ninja Foodi Dual Zone Air Fryer

This section describes the processes to follow when air frying, air broiling, roasting, reheating, dehydrating, and baking when using the Ninja Foodi Dual Zone Air Fryer equipment:

Air Fry

How to use the air fry functionality?
1. Put the crisper plate in position, then add all the ingredients into the drawer and fit it into the main unit.
2. The appliance will automatically put zone 1 on.

3. Click the AIR FRY function.
4. Use the TEMP arrows to set the appropriate temperature.
5. Use the TIME arrows to set the appropriate time.
6. Select the START/PAUSE function to initiate the process.
7. You can remove the drawer and flip, toss, or shake the food according to the recipe guidelines.
8. Once done, the equipment will beep and show the end signal on the display
9. Remove the food carefully and serve.

Air Broil

How to use the air fry functionality (AIR BROIL cannot be used in both zones at the same time?)

1. Put the crisper plate in position, then add all the ingredients into the drawer and fit it into the main unit.
2. The appliance will automatically put zone 1 on.
3. Click the AIR BROIL function.
4. Use the TEMP arrows to set the appropriate temperature.
5. Use the TIME arrows to set the appropriate time.
6. Select the START/PAUSE function to initiate the process.
7. You can remove the drawer and flip, toss, or shake the food according to the recipe guidelines.
8. Once done, the equipment will beep and show the end signal on the display
9. Remove the food carefully and serve.

Roast

You can roast chicken, beef, pork, and even vegetables in minutes with the Ninja Foodi Dual Zone Air Fryer. If possible, prepare the meats you want to roast in advance and store them in the freezer. When ready to cook, you simply pick and start the coking processes with your Ninja Foodi Dual Zone Air Fryer.

How to use the roast functionality?

For roasting your meals, follow the steps below:
1. Start by installing crisper plate in the drawer (optional), then place ingredients in the drawer, and insert drawer in unit.
2. The appliance will choose zone 1 automatically, then click on the ROAST button.
3. Use TEMP arrows to set the required temperature and time using the TIME arrows.

4. Click START/PAUSE to begin the cooking process.
5. Once cooked, you will hear the beep from the appliance, and then you will see the end signal on the display.
6. Remove the meals carefully and enjoy.

Reheat

Before reheating any food, ensure it is at room temperature. The Ninja Foodi Dual Zone Air Fryer is made with advanced technology that heats rapidly and distributes heat on the food evenly, ensuring it reheats well and faster. Besides, it gives the reheated food a good look, making it colorful for everyone. For reheating, follow the steps below:

How to use the reheat functionality?

1. Start by installing crisper plate in the drawer (optional), then place ingredients in the drawer, and insert drawer in unit.
2. By default, the unit will pock zone 1; you can select zone 2 if you want to.
3. Click the REHEAT functionality, then set the temperature with the TEMP arrows and time with the TIME arrows.
4. Click START/PAUSE to begin the reheating process
5. Once done, the unit will beep and display the end signal
6. Carefully remove the food and serve.

Dehydrate

With the Ninja Foodi Dual Zone Air Fryer, you can dehydrate foods faster. Ideally, you can dehydrate any food faster and evenly without getting burned.

How to use the dehydrate functionality?

For all the fruits, vegetables, nuts, and any other food, dehydrate using the following steps:

1. Put all the ingredients in the drawer, arranging them in a single layer, then set the crisper plate over the ingredients and add more ingredients on top.
2. The unit will automatically select zone 1, then press the DEHYDRATE function. Adjust the temperature settings with TEMP arrows and time settings with TIME arrows.
3. Click START/PAUSE to start the process.
4. You will hear the beep sound once done, and the display will show "END."
5. Remove the ingredients carefully.

Fundamentals of Ninja Foodi Dual Zone Air Fryer | 9

Bake

With the Ninja Foodi Dual Zone Air Fryer, you can bake cakes, biscuits, muffins, cookies, or any other treat you want to make. But this cooking function is not available on all models.

How to use the bake functionality?
1. Start by installing crisper plate in the drawer (optional), then place ingredients in the drawer, and insert drawer in unit.
2. The appliance will select zone 1 automatically. Click the BAKE function.
3. Set the temperatures by adjusting the TEMP arrows. (If you are using recipes from a traditional oven, reduce the temperatures by 25°F).
4. Use TIME arrows to adjust the appropriate time setting, then click the START/PAUSE function to start the cooking process.
5. Once cooked, the unit will beep and display the END signal.
6. Remove the meals carefully and serve.

Cooking Tips

When cooking using the Ninja Foodi Dual Zone Air Fryer, the following tips will always come in handy:
- If you click the START/PAUSE function when using the smart finish, the cooking process will stop on both zones. Therefore, select the same option again to continue the cooking process.
- You can always change the time and temperature settings during the cooking process using the arrows to ensure the final results are compelling.
- Always select the first time zone first when you want to pause the cooking process, then click the START/PAUSE button.
- Don't over-stack food. Make sure everything is in a single layer for even cooking.
- Add about a tablespoon of cooking when making veggies for a perfect finish.
- During the cooking process, make it a habit to shake, toss, or flip the meals at least two times for even cooking.
- For crunchier foods, use the crisper plates.
- Make sure you bread the food appropriately to avoid wet, battered foods. Therefore, first, use the flour, then egg and bread crumbs, ensuring you press the

bread crumbs to stick well.
- Once the cooking process is over, use kitchen tongs or appropriate kitchen equipment to remove the hot food carefully to avoid burning.
- Make it a habit to always monitor the cooking process progress. Check the chart showing details of cooking different meals.
- Avoid using metal equipment or tools when handling other parts and accessories of the Ninja Foodi Dual Zone Air Fryer, as they could damage the accessories, making them lose the original coating. You can use tongs with silicon tips or simply tip move the meals directly on the place from the unit.
- Always ensure the food reaches the required temperature when cooking to evade issues due to food poisoning and such. Therefore, you shouldn't miss an instant-read thermometer, especially in the case of meats.
- If you are converting recipes for the traditional ovens, ensure you adjust the temperature settings by reducing the settings by 25°F. Ideally, check for doneness continuously.
- You can secure pieces of food with toothpicks to avoid being blown away during the cooking process.
- Do not overload the air fryer baskets. This can damage the appliance. Besides, the food won't cook evenly.
- The food shouldn't touch the heating elements.
- Above all, don't forget to read and refer to the user guide whenever you feel stuck or don't know the process well.

Helpful Safety Guidelines

While you are looking forward to the tips that will help you with the cooking processes, we cannot just evade the need to describe safety measures and guidelines to always familiarize yourself with. Below are the ultimate safety guidelines to observe when using the Ninja Foodi Dual Zone Air Fryer appliance.
- Don't skip reading the user manual for all the safety precautions when operating the unit.
- People who understand how to use or have read the guide are the only ones to operate the unit.

- Don't allow children to operate or play with the equipment unsupervised.
- Don't situate the Ninja Foodi Dual Zone Air Fryer near heated surfaces like burners and ovens. Again, avoid damp or wet areas when fitting your appliance in the kitchen.
- Remember to take caution when using the equipment, more so when kids are around.
- Put the device on a heat-resistant and leveled surface, leaving enough space all around.
- Keep off any flammable materials.
- Always ensure both air inlet and air outlets are clear without any obstructions.
- Avoid moving or transferring the unit when the cooking process is on.
- Don't use the extension cord on the air fryer to avoid tripping or related accidents.
- Don't soak the whole unit, the plug, and the cord in any liquid
- Only use dry crisper plates and baskets in the unit
- Always try your best to use parts and accessories provided by the manufacturer. If any of the parts get damaged, you can always purchase more from the main dealers.
- Don't situate hot baskets over the appliance. In any case, you shouldn't put anything on top of the unit.
- The baskets are made for air fryers only. Therefore, do not attempt to divert and use them on grills, burners, microwaves, and ovens.
- Always check if the baskets and other accessories are well-fitted before pressing the start button.
- Don't use the air fryer without the baskets attached
- Don't forget to use protective gear such as insulated gloves, oven mittens, or kitchen towels when removing cooked food from the unit to avoid burns.

- Don't use the air fryer for outdoor services.
- Always remember to unplug the device before you begin the cleaning process.
- The power cord shouldn't hang over the kitchen counter
- If you notice some damaged parts and accessories of the Ninja Foodi Dual Zone Air Fryer, do not use the appliance unless it is inspected by experts first.
- Unplug the unit immediately if you notice any black or strange smoke from the unit. Again, wait until the smoke is over to remove the parts and accessories.

Cleaning and Maintenance Tips

As a way of ensuring the Ninja Foodi Dual Zone Air Fryer serves you well and last longer, you should ensure it is well-maintained, and part of the plan to ensure this is regular cleaning. In the guide, the appliance has guidelines on how to clean and maintain it properly.

The tips below will help you with the cleaning and maintenance processes:

- The baskets and crisper plates are dishwasher-friendly. However, it is better to hand wash the baskets with warm and soapy water to maintain their original coating.
- Make it a habit to always clean the appliance after every use.
- Unplug the unit from the socket before washing.
- Only clean the appliance after cooling it down.
- Never immerse the whole unit and the electrical cord in water or any other liquid.
- Use a clean and dump cloth to wipe the exterior of the unit.
- Avoid harsh abrasives on the baskets and the crisper plates. Also, do not scrape the baskets and crisper plates to ensure they maintain their original coating for long.
- Always inspect the whole unit for possible cracks and damages.

Straight from the Store

When unboxing the Ninja Foodi Dual Zone Air Fryer, you will see an elegant and sophisticated kitchen appliance. It has a smooth black and chrome appearance, making it desirable, especially when fitted on your kitchen counter.

It comes with the following accessories:
- The main unit
- Nonstick drawers
- Air outlet
- Nonstick crisper plates for the drawers
- Control panel
- Air intake vent

Two cooking drawers, with each drawer big enough to hold up to 7.6 liters. The depth of the drawers is big enough and can cook up to 12 muffins, 35 oz. Chicken, and 1 pound of sweet potatoes. The drawers are designed to slide effortlessly with steady handles that are easy to insert and remove without getting damaged. The crisper plates enhance the browning of food because they enable even circulation of air around the food, thus giving it a golden and crispy texture. Again, the crisper plates help prevent food from clinging to the bottom of the compartment, thus making it easy to remove for cleaning purposes.

The other parts are the functionalities to use according to the meal you are preparing. The display screen is good enough, showing you the progress of the meal you are making. Ideally, the Ninja Foodi Dual Zone Air Fryer is a must-have-kitchen appliance, especially if you are a busy person who wants healthy meals within a short time.

Frequently Asked Questions & Notes

Can I use other cookware in my Ninja Foodi Dual Zone Air Fryer?
Yes. Apart from the parts and accessories that come with the unit, you can use the baking sheets and trays used in a basic oven. However, nonstick options would be better to ensure even cooking. In any case, it could be better to use the cookware that comes with the unit for best results.

Can buttered food be cooked in the Ninja Foodi Dual Zone Air Fryer?
Yes, you can prepare buttered foods in your ninja dual air fryer. However, since buttered food doesn't hold up long enough, you might need to add some more oil than other foods. Still, the oil shouldn't be too much if you want a crispy texture of the meal.

What oils are the best in the Ninja Foodi Dual Zone Air Fryer?
For best oil results, always check the smoke point. Oils with higher smoke points are best in the air fryer. Examples include avocado, peanut, and grapeseed oil. Oils that have low smoke points, such as vegetable oil and extra virgin olive oil, don't work best with the Ninja Foodi Dual Zone Air Fryer.

What makes food to be undercooked or overcooked?
At times, it can be difficult to rule whether the food is overcooked or undercooked, especially just by looking at it. Especially for meats, it is always advisable to insert the thermometer throughout the cooking process. Keep checking the temperatures to know when the food has fully cooked. This will also avoid overcooking.

Should I get worried about contamination or food poisoning issues when cooking different meals in different zones?
You shouldn't get worried about the different zones. Each zone is independent, with fans and space. Therefore, issues with food contamination will never arise when using the Ninja Foodi Dual Zone Air Fryer.

4-Week Meal Plan

Week 1

Day 1:
Breakfast: Flavourful Greek Omelet with Cheese
Lunch: Roasted Kabocha Squash
Snack: Cheese Broccoli Tots
Dinner: Easy Gingered Chicken Drumsticks
Dessert: Chocolate Cookies

Day 2:
Breakfast: Crispy Spinach-Cheese Balls
Lunch: Roasted Dijon Asparagus
Snack: Healthy Broccoli Hash Brown
Dinner: Roasted Spiced Lamb Cutlets
Dessert: Easy Popcorn Chicken Balls

Day 3:
Breakfast: Delicious Scrambled Egg Muffins
Lunch: Quick Brussels Sprouts
Snack: Creamy Broccoli Puree
Dinner: Fried Prawns Skewers
Dessert: Flavourful Fluffy Chocolate Cake

Day 4:
Breakfast: Crispy Onion Rings with Mayo Dip
Lunch: Flavourful Cheese Cauliflower Casserole
Snack: Easy Aubergine Bites
Dinner: BBQ Chicken Wings
Dessert: Yummy Chocolate Brownies

Day 5:
Breakfast: Spicy Pickle Relish Deviled Eggs
Lunch: Crispy Broccoli Tots
Snack: Roasted Brussels Sprouts
Dinner: Delicious Beef Bulgogi Burgers
Dessert: Sweet Espresso Brownies

Day 6:
Breakfast: Cauliflower Egg Bake
Lunch: Easy Roasted Asparagus
Snack: Crispy Red Beetroot Chips
Dinner: Flavourful Tuna Patties
Dessert: Soft Blueberry Cupcakes

Day 7:
Breakfast: Air Fried Cheese Sticks with Low-Carb Ketchup
Lunch: Fried Potato Cubes
Snack: Honeyed Chicken Wings
Dinner: Dijon Chuck Eye Steak
Dessert: Homemade Double Chocolate Brownies

Week 2

Day 1:
Breakfast: Traditional Scotch Eggs
Lunch: Tasty Cheese Veggie Quesadilla
Snack: Quick Tortilla Chips
Dinner: Roasted Chicken Thighs
Dessert: Crispy Chocolate Chips Cookies

Day 2:
Breakfast: Chocolate & Courgette Muffins
Lunch: Simple Cheesy Courgette Bake
Snack: Simple Cheese-Stuffed Mushrooms
Dinner: Quick Peppermint Lamb Chops
Dessert: Fresh Blackberry Muffins

Day 3:
Breakfast: Crispy Cheese Mushroom Balls
Lunch: Flavourful Cheese Cauliflower Casserole
Snack: Spicy Juicy Chicken Drumsticks
Dinner: Spicy Prawns and Cherry Tomato Kebabs
Dessert: Simple Spanish Churros

Day 4:
Breakfast: Simple Bagels
Lunch: Roasted Dijon Asparagus
Snack: Sweet-and-Spicy Spare Ribs
Dinner: Crispy Chicken Nuggets
Dessert: Basic Vanilla Cupcakes

Day 5:
Breakfast: Homemade Black Bean Arepas
Lunch: Roasted Kabocha Squash
Snack: Cheese Broccoli Tots
Dinner: Pork Patties with Blue Cheese
Dessert: Tasty Chocolate Lava Cake

Day 6:
Breakfast: Flavourful Greek Omelet with Cheese
Lunch: Easy Roasted Asparagus
Snack: Sweet-and-Spicy Spare Ribs
Dinner: Crispy Fish Fillets
Dessert: Delicious Chocolate Mascarpone Cake

Day 7:
Breakfast: Crispy Onion Rings with Mayo Dip
Lunch: Crispy Broccoli Tots
Snack: Healthy Broccoli Hash Brown
Dinner: Fajita Meatball Lettuce Wraps
Dessert: Chocolate Cookies

Week 3

Day 1:
Breakfast: Spicy Pickle Relish Deviled Eggs
Lunch: Fried Potato Cubes
Snack: Easy Aubergine Bites
Dinner: Roasted Thanksgiving Turkey Breast
Dessert: Easy Popcorn Chicken Balls

Day 2:
Breakfast: Cheesy Broccoli Balls
Lunch: Quick Brussels Sprouts
Snack: Creamy Broccoli Puree
Dinner: Garlic Lamb Chops
Dessert: Yummy Chocolate Brownies

Day 3:
Breakfast: Cauliflower Egg Bake
Lunch: Tasty Cheese Veggie Quesadilla
Snack: Roasted Brussels Sprouts
Dinner: French Sea Bass with Sauce
Dessert: Flavourful Fluffy Chocolate Cake

Day 4:
Breakfast: Air Fried Cheese Sticks with Low-Carb Ketchup
Lunch: Simple Cheesy Courgette Bake
Snack: Crispy Red Beetroot Chips
Dinner: Crispy Chicken Tenders
Dessert: Sweet Espresso Brownies

Day 5:
Breakfast: Chocolate & Courgette Muffins
Lunch: Roasted Dijon Asparagus
Snack: Honeyed Chicken Wings
Dinner: Cheese Black and Blue Burgers
Dessert: Soft Blueberry Cupcakes

Day 6:
Breakfast: Traditional Scotch Eggs
Lunch: Flavourful Cheese Cauliflower Casserole
Snack: Quick Tortilla Chips
Dinner: Simple Salmon Patties
Dessert: Homemade Double Chocolate Brownies

Day 7:
Breakfast: Simple Bagels
Lunch: Roasted Kabocha Squash
Snack: Simple Cheese-Stuffed Mushrooms
Dinner: Lamb Meatballs
Dessert: Fresh Blackberry Muffins

Week 4

Day 1:
Breakfast: Homemade Black Bean Arepas
Lunch: Crispy Broccoli Tots
Snack: Spicy Juicy Chicken Drumsticks
Dinner: Healthy Roasted Turkey Breasts
Dessert: Crispy Chocolate Chips Cookies

Day 2:
Breakfast: Crispy Spinach-Cheese Balls
Lunch: Easy Roasted Asparagus
Snack: Sweet-and-Spicy Spare Ribs
Dinner: Air Fried Marjoram Lamb Chops
Dessert: Simple Spanish Churros

Day 3:
Breakfast: Delicious Scrambled Egg Muffins
Lunch: Quick Brussels Sprouts
Snack: Cheese Broccoli Tots
Dinner: Baked Salmon Steaks with Butter and Wine
Dessert: Basic Vanilla Cupcakes

Day 4:
Breakfast: Flavourful Greek Omelet with Cheese
Lunch: Fried Potato Cubes
Snack: Healthy Broccoli Hash Brown
Dinner: Roasted Turkey Sausage with Cauliflower
Dessert: Tasty Chocolate Lava Cake

Day 5:
Breakfast: Crispy Onion Rings with Mayo Dip
Lunch: Tasty Cheese Veggie Quesadilla
Snack: Easy Aubergine Bites
Dinner: Homemade Cheesy Mushroom Burgers
Dessert: Delicious Chocolate Mascarpone Cake

Day 6:
Breakfast: Spicy Pickle Relish Deviled Eggs
Lunch: Simple Cheesy Courgette Bake
Snack: Creamy Broccoli Puree
Dinner: Roasted Lemony Prawns
Dessert: Chocolate Cookies

Day 7:
Breakfast: Air Fried Cheese Sticks with Low-Carb Ketchup
Lunch: Roasted Dijon Asparagus
Snack: Roasted Brussels Sprouts
Dinner: BBQ Chicken Wings
Dessert: Easy Popcorn Chicken Balls

Chapter 1 Breakfast

- 19 Delicious Scrambled Egg Muffins
- 19 Crispy Spinach-Cheese Balls
- 20 Crispy Cheese Mushroom Balls
- 20 Flavourful Greek Omelet with Cheese
- 21 Crispy Onion Rings with Mayo Dip
- 21 Spicy Pickle Relish Deviled Eggs
- 22 Air Fried Cheese Sticks with Low-Carb Ketchup
- 22 Cheesy Broccoli Balls
- 23 Cauliflower Egg Bake
- 23 Traditional Scotch Eggs
- 24 Chocolate & Courgette Muffins
- 24 Simple Bagels
- 25 Homemade Black Bean Arepas

Delicious Scrambled Egg Muffins

⏰ **Prep: 20 minutes**　🍲 **Cook: 16 minutes**　📚 6

Preparation:

1. Combine the sausage, eggs, shallots, black pepper, garlic, salt, and cayenne pepper in a mixing dish.
2. Spoon the mixture into 6 standard-size muffin cups with paper liners.
3. Transfer the muffin cups into the basket in zone 1.
4. Select BAKE mode, adjust the cooking temperature to 170°C and set the cooking time to 16 minutes.
5. Press the START/PAUSE button to begin cooking.
6. Top the muffins with cheese halfway through the cooking time.
7. Enjoy.

Ingredients:

150g smoked turkey sausage, chopped
6 eggs, lightly beaten
2 tablespoons shallots, finely chopped
2 garlic cloves, minced
Sea salt and ground black pepper, to taste
1 teaspoon cayenne pepper
150g Monterey Jack cheese, shredded

Per Serving: Calories 234; Fat 15.76g; Sodium 438mg; Carbs 5.38g; Fibre 0.4g; Sugar 0.99g; Protein 17.62g

Crispy Spinach-Cheese Balls

⏰ **Prep: 15 minutes**　🍲 **Cook: 15 minutes**　📚 4

Preparation:

1. Pour all the ingredients into a food processor or blender, and then puree the ingredients until it becomes dough.
2. Roll the dough into small balls.
3. Insert the crisper plates in the baskets. Divide the dough balls the baskets in zone 1 and zone 2.
4. Select AIR FRY mode, adjust the cooking temperature to 155°C and set the cooking time to 12 minutes.
5. Press the MATCH COOK button and copy the zone 1 settings to zone 2.
6. Press the START/PAUSE button to begin cooking.
7. Serve hot.

Ingredients:

60ml milk
2 eggs
100g cheese
60g spinach, torn into pieces
35g flaxseed meal
½ teaspoon baking powder
2 tablespoons rapeseed oil
Salt and ground black pepper, to taste

Per Serving: Calories 219; Fat 15.86g; Sodium 630mg; Carbs 10.04g; Fibre 2.3g; Sugar 3.25g; Protein 10.76g

Crispy Cheese Mushroom Balls

⏰ Prep: 30 minutes   🍲 Cook: 25 minutes   🍽 4

Preparation:

1. Blitz the cauliflower florets in your food processor until they're crumbled.
2. Heat the oil in a saucepan over a moderate heat; add the cauliflower, garlic, onions, and chili pepper and cook them until tender.
3. Throw in the mushrooms and fry until they are fragrant and the liquid has almost evaporated.
4. Add the vegetable stock and boil for 18 minutes.
5. Add the salt, black pepper, Swiss cheese, and beaten egg; mix them to combine.
6. Allow the mixture to cool completely. Shape the mixture into balls. Dip the balls in the grated parmesan cheese.
7. Insert the crisper plates in the baskets. Divide the balls between the baskets in zone 1 and zone 2.
8. Select AIR FRY mode, adjust the cooking temperature to 205°C and set the cooking time to 7 minutes.
9. Press the MATCH COOK button and copy the zone 1 settings to zone 2.
10. Press the START/PAUSE button to begin cooking. 11. Serve hot.

Ingredients:

1½ tablespoons olive oil
100g cauliflower florets
3 garlic cloves, peeled and minced
½ yellow onion, finely chopped
1 small-sized red chili pepper, seeded and minced
120ml roasted vegetable stock
200g white mushrooms, finely chopped
Sea salt and ground black pepper, or more to taste
50g Swiss cheese, grated
50g parmesan cheese
1 egg, beaten

Per Serving: Calories 219; Fat 15.86g; Sodium 630mg; Carbs 10.04g; Fibre 2.3g; Sugar 3.25g; Protein 10.76g

Flavourful Greek Omelet with Cheese

⏰ Prep: 17 minutes   🍲 Cook: 15 minutes   🍽 2

Preparation:

1. Combine all of the ingredients in a large bowl until everything is well incorporated.
2. Transfer the mixture to the basket in zone 1.
3. Select AIR FRY mode, adjust the cooking temperature to 160°C and set the cooking time to 15 minutes.
4. Press the START/PAUSE button to begin cooking. 5. Serve warm.

Ingredients:

65g Halloumi cheese, sliced
2 teaspoons garlic paste
2 teaspoons fresh chopped rosemary
4 well-whisked eggs
2 peppers, seeded and chopped
1½ tablespoons fresh basil, chopped
3 tablespoons onions, chopped
Fine sea salt and ground black pepper, to taste

Per Serving: Calories 251; Fat 15.46g; Sodium 1239mg; Carbs 10.64g; Fibre 1.3g; Sugar 5.67g; Protein 17.78g

Crispy Onion Rings with Mayo Dip

⏰ Prep: 25 minutes   🍲 Cook: 15 minutes   📚 3

Preparation:

1. Cut off the top 1 cm of the Vidalia onion; peel your onion and place it cut-side down.
2. Starting 1 cm from the root, cut the onion in half. Make a second cut that splits each half in two.
3. You will have 4 quarters held together by the root.
4. Repeat these cuts, splitting the 4 quarters to yield eighths; then, you should split them again until you have 16 evenly spaced cuts.
5. Turn the onion over and gently separate the outer pieces.
6. In a mixing bowl, thoroughly mix the almond flour and spices. In a separate bowl, whisk the milk and eggs.
7. Dip the onion rings into the egg mixture, followed by the almond flour mixture.
8. Insert the crisper plates in the baskets. Divide the onion rings between the baskets in zone 1 and zone 2.
9. Select AIR FRY mode, adjust the cooking temperature to 190°C and set the cooking time to 15 minutes.
10. Press the MATCH COOK button and copy the zone 1 settings to zone 2.
11. Press the START/PAUSE button to begin cooking.
12. Whisk the remaining ingredients to make the mayo dip.
13. Serve the onion rings with mayo dip.

Ingredients:

1 large onion
50g almond flour
1 teaspoon salt
½ teaspoon ground black pepper
1 teaspoon cayenne pepper
½ teaspoon dried thyme
½ teaspoon dried oregano
½ teaspoon ground cumin
2 eggs
4 tablespoons milk
Mayo Dip
3 tablespoons mayonnaise
3 tablespoons sour cream
1 tablespoon horseradish, drained
Salt and freshly ground black pepper, to taste

Per Serving: Calories 149; Fat 9.88g; Sodium 976mg; Carbs 9.14g; Fibre 1.6g; Sugar 4.26g; Protein 6.59g

Spicy Pickle Relish Deviled Eggs

⏰ Prep: 20 minutes   🍲 Cook: 15 minutes   📚 3

Preparation:

1. Insert the crisper plate in the basket in zone 1, and transfer the eggs to it.
2. Select AIR FRY mode, adjust the cooking temperature to 130°C and set the cooking time to 15 minutes.
3. Press the START/PAUSE button to begin cooking.
4. Transfer the cooked eggs to an ice-cold water bath to stop the cooking. Peel the eggs under cold running water. Then slice them into halves.
5. Mash the egg yolks with the mayo, sweet pickle relish, and salt; spoon yolk mixture into egg whites.
6. Arrange on a nice serving platter and garnish with the mixed peppercorns.

Ingredients:

5 eggs
2 tablespoons mayonnaise
2 tablespoons pickle relish
Sea salt, to taste
½ teaspoon mixed peppercorns, crushed

Per Serving: Calories 150; Fat 10.2g; Sodium 314mg; Carbs 4.4g; Fibre 0.2g; Sugar 3.29g; Protein 9.84g

Air Fried Cheese Sticks with Low-Carb Ketchup

⏰ Prep: 15 minutes 🍲 Cook: 6 minutes 📚 4

Preparation:

1. Add the flour in a shallow dish.
2. In a separate dish, whisk the eggs.
3. Mix the parmesan cheese and Cajun seasoning in a third dish.
4. Dredge the cheese sticks in the flour and then dip in into the egg. Press the cheese sticks into the parmesan mixture, coating them evenly.
5. Insert the crisper plates in the baskets. Divide the cheese sticks between the baskets in zone 1 and zone 2.
6. Select AIR FRY mode, adjust the cooking temperature to 190°C and set the cooking time to 6 minutes.
7. Press the MATCH COOK button and copy the zone 1 settings to zone 2.
8. Press the START/PAUSE button to begin cooking.
9. Serve the cheese sticks with ketchup.

Ingredients:

30g coconut flour
25g almond flour
2 eggs
50g Parmesan cheese, grated
1 tablespoon Cajun seasonings
8 cheese sticks, kid-friendly
60g ketchup, low-carb

Per Serving: Calories 322; Fat 24.58g; Sodium 799mg; Carbs 4.69g; Fibre 0.5g; Sugar 1.08g; Protein 20g

Cheesy Broccoli Balls

⏰ Prep: 25 minutes 🍲 Cook: 16 minutes 📚 4

Preparation:

1. Add the broccoli to your food processor and pulse until the consistency resembles rice. Stir in the remaining ingredients; mix until everything is well combined.
2. Shape the mixture into bite-sized balls.
3. Insert the crisper plates in the baskets. Divide the balls between the baskets in zone 1 and zone 2.
4. Select AIR FRY mode, adjust the cooking temperature to 190°C and set the cooking time to 16 minutes.
5. Press the MATCH COOK button and copy the zone 1 settings to zone 2.
6. Press the START/PAUSE button to begin cooking.
7. Flip the balls halfway through the cooking time.
8. Serve the dish with cocktail sticks and tomato ketchup on the side.

Ingredients:

225g broccoli
225g Romano cheese, grated
2 garlic cloves, minced
1 shallot, chopped
4 eggs, beaten
2 tablespoons butter, at room temperature
½ teaspoon paprika
¼ teaspoon dried basil
Sea salt and ground black pepper, to taste

Per Serving: Calories 351; Fat 25.55g; Sodium 940mg; Carbs 5.11g; Fibre 1.8g; Sugar 1.04g; Protein 25.63g

Cauliflower Egg Bake

🕐 **Prep:** 5 minutes 🍲 **Cook:** 20 minutes 🎚 4

Preparation:

1. Install a crisper plate in the Zone 1 basket and grease with the butter.
2. In a medium bowl, whisk the eggs with salt, paprika, and pepper. Place the cauliflower florets in the bottom of the basket, then add the egg mix, toss well. Insert the basket in the unit.
3. Select Zone 1, select BAKE, set the temperature to 160°C, and set the time for 20 minutes. Press START/PAUSE to begin cooking.
4. When cooking is complete, divide between plates and serve for breakfast.

Ingredients:

180 g cauliflower florets, separated
4 eggs, whisked
1 teaspoon sweet paprika
2 tablespoons butter, melted
A pinch of salt and black pepper

Per Serving: Calories 200; Fat 15.64g; Sodium 165mg; Carbs 5.05g; Fibre 1.4g; Sugar 2.31g; Protein 10.36g

Traditional Scotch Eggs

🕐 **Prep:** 15 minutes 🍲 **Cook:** 13 minutes 🎚 4

Preparation:

1. Mix together beef mince and garlic powder in a medium bowl. Add almond flour, cayenne pepper, and curry powder. Stir the mixture until homogenous.
2. Then, wrap the peeled eggs in the beef mince mixture. You will get some meatballs. Coat every ball in the beaten egg and then sprinkle with coconut flakes.
3. Install a crisper plate in the Zone 1 basket and spray the air fryer basket with cooking spray. Place the meat eggs inside. Then insert the basket in the unit.
4. Select Zone 1, select AIR FRY, set the temperature to 205°C, and set the time for 13 minutes. Press START/PAUSE to begin cooking.
5. Carefully flip the scotch eggs on another side after 7 minutes of cooking.

Ingredients:

4 medium eggs, hard-boiled, peeled
225 g beef mince
1 teaspoon garlic powder
¼ teaspoon cayenne pepper
25 g coconut flakes
¼ teaspoon curry powder
1 egg, beaten
1 tablespoon almond flour
Cooking spray

Per Serving: Calories 314; Fat 25.94g; Sodium 138mg; Carbs 1.6g; Fibre 0.3g; Sugar 0.56g; Protein 17.2g

Chocolate & Courgette Muffins

⏰ Prep: 10 minutes 🍲 Cook: 36 minutes 📚 2

Preparation:

1. Mix the flaxseed with water in a small bowl.
2. Whisk together the whole wheat pastry flour, plain flour, baking soda, cocoa powder, cinnamon and salt in a small bowl.
3. Add the rapeseed oil, sugar, vanilla extract, lemon juice, and flaxseed mixture to mix well. Add the courgette and chocolate chips. Place the batter into the muffin cups.
4. Install a crisper plate in the Zone 1 basket. Working in batches, place 6 muffin cups in the basket, and insert the basket into the unit. The unit will default to Zone
1. Select BAKE. Set the temperature to 130°C and set the time to 18 minutes. Press the START/PAUSE button to cook until a toothpick coming out.
5. When cooking is complete, remove the cups from the basket and let the muffins cool for 10 minutes before serving.

Ingredients:

1 tbsp ground flaxseed
3 tbsp water
60 g plain flour
35 g whole wheat pastry flour
25 g unsweetened cocoa powder
¼ tsp baking soda
¼ tsp salt
¼ tsp ground cinnamon
100 g granulated sugar
60 ml rapeseed oil
½ tsp pure vanilla extract
½ tsp freshly squeezed lemon juice
35 g grated courgette
50 g vegan chocolate chips

Per Serving: Calories 768; Fat 32.38g; Sodium 515mg; Carbs116.79 g; Fibre 9.2g; Sugar 62.28g; Protein 9.8g

Simple Bagels

⏰ Prep: 10 minutes 🍲 Cook: 12 minutes 📚 4

Preparation:

1. Mix together the baking powder, flour and salt in a large bowl. Add the yogurt to stir with a spatula until a loose dough shapes.
2. Remove the dough onto a lightly floured board. Lightly knead the dough until it comes together.
3. Divide the dough in half and then into 4 equally sized pieces. Knead each piece of dough into a ball and gently press to flatten.
4. Cut a hole in the centre with a small ring mold or a butter knife. Spray nonstick cooking spray on top of the dough with. Season with 1 to 2 teaspoons of seasoning over each disc.
5. Install a crisper plate in the Zone 1 basket, place the dough in the basket, and insert the basket into the unit. The unit will default to Zone
1. Select BAKE. Set the temperature to 160°C and set the time to 12 minutes. Press the START/PAUSE button to cook until puffed and golden brown.
6. When the cook is complete, transfer the bagels to a wire rack to cool slightly. Serve. Slice, toast, and top as desired.

Ingredients:

120 g plain flour, plus more
2 tsp baking powder
½ tsp salt
150g unsweetened dairy-free yogurt (soy recommended)
Everything bagel seasoning

Per Serving: Calories 198; Fat 0.8g; Sodium 1677mg; Carbs38.98 g; Fibre 2.2g; Sugar1.76 g; Protein 8.94g

24 | Chapter 1 Breakfast

Homemade Black Bean Arepas

⏲ **Prep:** 10 minutes   🍲 **Cook:** 15 minutes   📚 2

Preparation:

1. Warm 2 teaspoons of olive oil at medium heat in a small frying pan. Add the onion and pepper. Sauté for about 5 minutes until slightly tender.
2. Add the cumin, beans and ½ teaspoon of salt to stir. Transfer the frying pan from the heat and set it aside to cool slightly.
3. Mix the semolina, water with 1 teaspoon of salt in a medium bowl. Mix well until a soft dough forms.
4. Knead the dough into a ball and divide into 4 equally sized pieces. Divide each piece in half and form each half into a small disc. Add 2 tablespoons of filling to the centre of the discs. Place the remaining discs on top and gently press the edges closed. Brush the discs on both sides with the remaining 1 tablespoon of olive oil.
5. Install a crisper plate in the Zone 1 basket, place the discs in the basket, and insert the basket into the unit. The unit will default to Zone
1. Select BAKE. Set the temperature to 195°Cand set the time to 15 minutes. Press the START/PAUSE button to cook until crispy.
6. When the cooking is complete, transfer to a serving plate and let cool slightly. Serve.

Ingredients:

2 tsp plus 1 tbsp olive oil
40 g diced red onion
45 g diced pepper (any colour)
½ tsp ground cumin
1½ tsp salt, divided
65 g canned black beans, rinsed and drained
120 g semolina
240 ml water

Per Serving: Calories 423; Fat 6.37g; Sodium 1755mg; Carbs 79.61g; Fibre 7.2g; Sugar 2.69g; Protein 11.19g

Chapter 2 Vegetables and Sides

27 Roasted Dijon Asparagus
27 Flavourful Cheese Cauliflower Casserole
28 Roasted Kabocha Squash
28 Easy Roasted Asparagus
29 Crispy Broccoli Tots
29 Quick Brussels Sprouts
30 Fried Potato Cubes
30 Tasty Cheese Veggie Quesadilla
31 Simple Cheesy Courgette Bake

Roasted Dijon Asparagus

⏱ **Prep: 5 minutes**   🍲 **Cook: 15 minutes**   🍽 **4**

Preparation:

1. In the shallow bowl, mix Dijon mustard with olive oil, and lemon juice.
2. Mix asparagus with mustard mixture.
3. Insert the crisper plate in the basket in zone 1, and transfer the asparagus mixture to it.
4. Select AIR FRY mode, adjust the cooking temperature to 205°C and set the cooking time to 12 minutes.
5. Press the START/PAUSE button to begin cooking.
6. After 10 minutes of cooking time, toss the asparagus.
7. Serve hot. Sprinkle with Parmesan cheese if desired.

Ingredients:

455g asparagus, trimmed
2 tablespoons Dijon mustard
1 tablespoon olive oil
1 teaspoon lemon juice

Per Serving: Calories 57; Fat 3.77g; Sodium 88mg; Carbs 4.94g; Fibre 2.7g; Sugar 2.24g; Protein 2.79g

Flavourful Cheese Cauliflower Casserole

⏱ **Prep: 10 minutes**   🍲 **Cook: 30 minutes**   🍽 **4**

Preparation:

1. Mix heavy cream with eggs and pour the liquid over the cheese.
2. Mix cauliflower with coconut oil.
3. Arrange the cauliflower into the baskets in single layer.
4. Top them with coriander and cheese, and pour the egg mixture over them.
5. Select ROAST mode, adjust the cooking temperature to 180°C and set the cooking time to 30 minutes.
6. Press the MATCH COOK button and copy the zone 1 settings to zone 2.
7. Press the START/PAUSE button to begin cooking.
8. Serve hot.

Ingredients:

3 tablespoons coconut oil, melted
240g heavy cream
2 eggs, beaten
200g Monterey Jack cheese, shredded
180g cauliflower, chopped
1 teaspoon dried coriander

Per Serving: Calories 482; Fat 43.53g; Sodium 455mg; Carbs 4.11g; Fibre 1.1g; Sugar 2.27g; Protein 20.56g

Roasted Kabocha Squash

⏰ **Prep: 10 minutes**   🍲 **Cook: 15 minutes**   📚 **4**

Preparation:

1. Cut the squash into cubes and sprinkle with onion powder, olive oil, and chili flakes.
2. Insert the crisper plate in the basket in zone 1, and transfer the squash cubes to it.
3. Select AIR FRY mode, adjust the cooking temperature to 185°C and set the cooking time to 12 minutes.
4. Press the START/PAUSE button to begin cooking.
5. Toss the cubes halfway through cooking.
6. Top the cooked meal with spring onions.

Ingredients:

250g Kabocha squash
1 teaspoon onion powder
25g spring onions, chopped
1 tablespoon olive oil
½ teaspoon chili flakes

Per Serving: Calories 63; Fat 3.52g; Sodium 14mg; Carbs 8.55g; Fibre 1.5g; Sugar 0.23g; Protein 0.81g

Easy Roasted Asparagus

⏰ **Prep: 5 minutes**   🍲 **Cook: 10 minutes**   📚 **4**

Preparation:

1. Spread asparagus spears on cookie sheet or cutting board.
2. Sprinkle the asparagus with tarragon, salt, and pepper.
3. Drizzle with 1 teaspoon of oil and roll the spears or mix by hand. If needed, add up to 1 more teaspoon of oil and mix again until all spears are lightly coated.
4. Insert the crisper plates in the baskets. Divide the food between the baskets in zone 1 and zone 2.
5. Select AIR FRY mode, adjust the cooking temperature to 200°C and set the cooking time to 10 minutes.
6. Press the MATCH COOK button and copy the zone 1 settings to zone 2.
7. Press the START/PAUSE button to begin cooking.
8. Stir the food halfway through cooking.
9. When done, the asparagus spears should be crisp-tender.

Ingredients:

1 bunch asparagus (approx. 455g), washed and trimmed
⅛ teaspoon dried tarragon, crushed
Salt and pepper
1 to 2 teaspoons extra-light olive oil

Per Serving: Calories 43; Fat 2.4g; Sodium 293mg; Carbs 4.62g; Fibre 2.5g; Sugar 2.14g; Protein 2.54g

Crispy Broccoli Tots

⏱ **Prep: 15 minutes** 🍲 **Cook: 10 minutes** 📚 **4-6**

Preparation:

1. Steam broccoli for 2 minutes. Rinse them in cold water, drain well, and chop finely.
2. In a large bowl, mix broccoli with all other ingredients except the oil.
3. Scoop out small portions of mixture and shape into 24 tots.
4. Insert the crisper plates in the baskets. Divide the tots between the baskets in zone 1 and zone 2.
5. Select AIR FRY mode, adjust the cooking temperature to 200°C and set the cooking time to 10 minutes.
6. Press the MATCH COOK button and copy the zone 1 settings to zone 2.
7. Press the START/PAUSE button to begin cooking.
8. Flip the tots halfway through cooking.
9. Serve hot.

Ingredients:

225g broccoli crowns
1 egg, beaten
⅛ teaspoon onion powder
¼ teaspoon salt
⅛ teaspoon pepper
2 tablespoons grated Parmesan cheese
30g panko breadcrumbs
Oil for misting

Per Serving: Calories 57; Fat 2.14g; Sodium 224mg; Carbs 6.1g; Fibre 1.5g; Sugar 0.64g; Protein 3.93g

Quick Brussels Sprouts

⏱ **Prep: 5 minutes** 🍲 **Cook: 5 minutes** 📚 **3**

Preparation:

1. Toss the Brussels sprouts and olive oil together.
2. Insert the crisper plates in the baskets.
3. Divide the food between the baskets in zone 1 and zone 2, and season them with salt and pepper.
4. Select AIR FRY mode, adjust the cooking temperature to 180°C and set the cooking time to 5 minutes.
5. Press the MATCH COOK button and copy the zone 1 settings to zone 2.
6. Press the START/PAUSE button to begin cooking.
7. When done, the edges should be lightly browned.

Ingredients:

1 (250g) package frozen Brussels sprouts, thawed and halved
2 teaspoons olive oil
Salt and pepper

Per Serving: Calories 62; Fat 3.35g; Sodium 396mg; Carbs 6.81g; Fibre 3.3g; Sugar 0g; Protein 3.19g

Fried Potato Cubes

⏰ Prep: 10 minutes   🍲 Cook: 25 minutes   ≋ 3-4

Preparation:

1. In a large bowl, combine the potatoes and oil thoroughly.
2. Insert the crisper plate in the basket in zone 1, and transfer the potatoes to it.
3. Select AIR FRY mode, adjust the cooking temperature to 200°C and set the cooking time to 25 minutes.
4. Press the START/PAUSE button to begin cooking.
5. Toss the potato cubes after 10 minutes of cooking time.
6. When cooked, season the potato cubes with salt and pepper. Sprinkle chopped coriander leaves for garnishing, if desired. Enjoy.

Ingredients:

1.3kg potatoes cut into 2.5cm cubes
½ teaspoon oil
Salt and pepper

Per Serving: Calories 267; Fat 0.88g; Sodium 20mg; Carbs 59.45g; Fibre 7.5g; Sugar 2.65g; Protein 6.87g

Tasty Cheese Veggie Quesadilla

⏰ Prep: 10 minutes   🍲 Cook: 9 minutes   ≋ 2

Preparation:

1. Heat the coconut oil in a medium skillet over medium heat. Add in the onion, pepper, and mushrooms and sauté until peppers become soft, about 4 minutes.
2. Place two tortillas on a work surface and sprinkle each with half of cheese. Sprinkle the sautéed veggies, remaining cheese on top, and top with the remaining two tortillas.
3. Install a crisper plate in the Zone 1 basket. Place quesadillas carefully in the basket. Then insert the basket in the unit.
4. Select Zone 1, select AIR FRY, set the temperature to 205°C, and set time for 5 minutes. Press START/PAUSE to begin cooking.
5. Flip the quesadillas halfway through the cooking process. Serve warm with avocado, sour cream, and salsa.

Ingredients:

1 tablespoon coconut oil
½ medium green pepper, seeded and chopped
30 g diced red onion
25 g chopped white mushrooms
4 flatbread dough tortillas
80 g shredded pepper jack cheese
½ medium avocado, peeled, pitted, and mashed
60 g full-fat sour cream
65 g mild salsa

Per Serving: Calories 623; Fat 33.2g; Sodium 1207mg; Carbs 62.17g; Fibre 6.8g; Sugar 6.51g; Protein 21.43g

Simple Cheesy Courgette Bake

Prep: 10 minutes   **Cook: 10 minutes**   **4**

Preparation:

1. Melt the butter in a large saucepan over medium heat. Add onion and sauté until it begins to soften, 1–3 minutes. Add garlic and sauté 30 seconds, then stir in cream and add cream cheese.
2. Remove the pan from heat and stir in Cheddar. Add the courgette and toss in the sauce, then transfer to a baking dish that fits the air fryer basket. Cover the dish with foil and place into the zone 1 basket. Then insert the basket in the unit.
3. Select Zone 1, select BAKE, set the temperature to 190°C, and set time for 8 minutes. Press START/PAUSE to begin cooking.
4. Remove the foil to brown the top in the last 2 minutes of cooking. Stir and serve.

Ingredients:

2 tablespoons salted butter
30 g diced white onion
½ teaspoon minced garlic
120 g heavy whipping cream
50 g full-fat cream cheese
100 g shredded sharp Cheddar cheese
2 medium courgette

Per Serving: Calories 244; Fat 21.63g; Sodium 292mg; Carbs 4.27g; Fibre 0.3g; Sugar 1.48g; Protein 8.6g

Chapter 3 Poultry

33   Easy Gingered Chicken Drumsticks
33   BBQ Chicken Wings
34   Roasted Chicken Thighs
34   Crispy Chicken Nuggets
35   Roasted Thanksgiving Turkey Breast
35   Crispy Chicken Tenders
36   Healthy Roasted Turkey Breasts
36   Roasted Turkey Sausage with Cauliflower
37   Refreshing Apple Vinegar Chicken Breast

Easy Gingered Chicken Drumsticks

⏰ **Prep: 5 minutes**   🍲 **Cook: 20 minutes**   📚 4

Preparation:

1. Coat the chicken drumsticks with onion powder, olive oil, ground cinnamon, and ground ginger.
2. Insert the crisper plates in the baskets. Divide the chicken drumsticks between the baskets in zone 1 and zone 2.
3. Select AIR FRY mode, adjust the cooking temperature to 190°C and set the cooking time to 20 minutes.
4. Press the MATCH COOK button and copy the zone 1 settings to zone 2.
5. Press the START/PAUSE button to begin cooking.
6. Garnish with rucola if desired. Serve hot.

Ingredients:

1 teaspoon ground ginger
½ teaspoon ground cinnamon
1 tablespoon olive oil
½ teaspoon onion powder
900g chicken drumsticks

Per Serving: Calories 398; Fat 24.27g; Sodium 241mg; Carbs 1.07g; Fibre 0.3g; Sugar 0.04g; Protein 41.09g

BBQ Chicken Wings

⏰ **Prep: 10 minutes**   🍲 **Cook: 20 minutes**   📚 4

Preparation:

1. Mix the chicken wings with BBQ sauce and olive oil.
2. Insert the crisper plate in the basket in zone 1, and transfer the chicken wings to it.
3. Select AIR FRY mode, adjust the cooking temperature to 190°C and set the cooking time to 18 minutes.
4. Press the START/PAUSE button to begin cooking.
5. Cook the chicken wings for 9 minutes on each side.

Ingredients:

900g chicken wings
240g keto BBQ sauce
1 teaspoon olive oil

Per Serving: Calories 315; Fat 9.26g; Sodium 642mg; Carbs 4.37g; Fibre 1.2g; Sugar 2.56g; Protein 50.83g

Roasted Chicken Thighs

⏱ **Prep: 15 minutes**   🍲 **Cook: 30 minutes**   📚 4

Preparation:

1. Rub the chicken thighs with taco seasonings and sprinkle with olive oil and apple cider vinegar.
2. Insert the crisper plate in the basket in zone 1, and transfer the chicken thighs to it.
3. Select AIR FRY mode, adjust the cooking temperature to 185°C and set the cooking time to 30 minutes.
4. Press the START/PAUSE button to begin cooking.
5. Flip the chicken thighs halfway through.
6. Transfer to a plate and garnish with fresh coriander leaves if desired. Serve.

Ingredients:

1 tablespoon taco seasonings
1 tablespoon apple cider vinegar
1 tablespoon olive oil
900g chicken thighs, skinless, boneless

Per Serving: Calories 539; Fat 41.05g; Sodium 339mg; Carbs 1.85g; Fibre 0.3g; Sugar 0.25g; Protein 37.56g

Crispy Chicken Nuggets

⏱ **Prep: 20 minutes**   🍲 **Cook: 10 minutes**   📚 4

Preparation:

1. Season each piece of the chicken with garlic salt, cayenne pepper, and black pepper.
2. In a mixing bowl, thoroughly combine the olive oil with protein powder and parmesan cheese.
3. Dredge each piece of chicken in the parmesan mixture.
4. Insert the crisper plates in the baskets. Divide the batter between the baskets in zone 1 and zone 2.
5. Select AIR FRY mode, adjust the cooking temperature to 200°C and set the cooking time to 8 minutes.
6. Press the MATCH COOK button and copy the zone 1 settings to zone 2.
7. Press the START/PAUSE button to begin cooking.
8. Serve hot with sauce you like.

Ingredients:

675g chicken tenderloins, cut into small pieces
½ teaspoon garlic salt
½ teaspoon cayenne pepper
¼ teaspoon black pepper, freshly cracked
4 tablespoons olive oil
2 scoops low-carb unflavoured protein powder
4 tablespoons Parmesan cheese, freshly grated

Per Serving: Calories 329; Fat 19.49g; Sodium 217mg; Carbs 1.05g; Fibre 0.1g; Sugar 0.03g; Protein 35.8g

Roasted Thanksgiving Turkey Breast

⏱ **Prep: 50 minutes** 🍲 **Cook: 50 minutes** 📚 6

Preparation:

1. Combine 2 tablespoons of butter, sage, salt, rosemary, and pepper; spread the mixture evenly over the surface of the turkey breast.
2. Insert the crisper plates in the baskets.
3. Divide the meat between the baskets in zone 1 and zone 2.
4. Select ROAST mode, adjust the cooking temperature to 180°C and set the cooking time to 48 minutes.
5. Press the MATCH COOK button and copy the zone 1 settings to zone 2.
6. Press the START/PAUSE button to begin cooking.
7. Flip the chicken breast halfway through cooking.
8. Flip the turkey breast after 20 minutes of cooking time and after 36 minutes of cooking time respectively.
9. While the turkey is roasting, whisk the other ingredients in a saucepan. After that, spread the gravy all over the turkey breast.
10. Let the turkey rest for a few minutes before carving.

Ingredients:

2 teaspoons butter, softened
1 teaspoon dried sage
2 sprigs rosemary, chopped
1 teaspoon salt
¼ teaspoon freshly ground black pepper, or more to taste
1 whole turkey breast
2 tablespoons turkey stock
2 tablespoons whole-grain mustard
1 tablespoon butter

Per Serving: Calories 381; Fat 8.39g; Sodium 711mg; Carbs 0.74g; Fibre 0.4g; Sugar 0.13g; Protein 71.35g

Crispy Chicken Tenders

⏱ **Prep: 80 minutes** 🍲 **Cook: 15 minutes** 📚 4

Preparation:

1. Place the buttermilk and chicken tenders in the mixing dish; gently stir to coat and let it soak for 1 hour.
2. Mix the coconut flour with flaxseed meal and all seasonings. Coat the soaked chicken tenders with the coconut flour mixture; now, dip them into the buttermilk.
3. Finally, dredge them in the coconut flour mixture.
4. Brush the prepared chicken tenders with sesame oil.
5. Insert the crisper plate in the basket in zone 1, and transfer the chicken thighs to it.
6. Select AIR FRY mode, adjust the cooking temperature to 185°C and set the cooking time to 15 minutes.
7. Press the START/PAUSE button to begin cooking.
8. Flip the chicken tenders once or twice during cooking.
9. Serve with sauce you like and enjoy.

Ingredients:

180ml of buttermilk
675g chicken tenders
60g coconut flour
2 tablespoons flaxseed meal
Salt, to your liking
½ teaspoon pink peppercorns, freshly cracked
1 teaspoon shallot powder
½ teaspoon cumin powder
1½ teaspoons smoked cayenne pepper
1 tablespoon sesame oil

Per Serving: Calories 516; Fat 28.15g; Sodium 880mg; Carbs 35.55g; Fibre 2g; Sugar 3.17g; Protein 30.75g

Healthy Roasted Turkey Breasts

⏱ **Prep: 25 minutes**   🍲 **Cook: 25 minutes**   📚 2

Preparation:

1. In a bowl, combine all ingredients together, making sure to coat turkey breast well.
2. Set them aside to marinate the turkey breast halves for at least 3 hours.
3. Insert the crisper plate in the basket in zone 1, and transfer the turkey breast halves to it.
4. Select ROAST mode, adjust the cooking temperature to 200°C and set the cooking time to 23 minutes.
5. Press the START/PAUSE button to begin cooking.
6. Flip the breast halves halfway through cooking.
7. Garnish with rosemary, if desired, and serve.

Ingredients:

½ tablespoon minced fresh parsley
1½ tablespoons Worcestershire sauce
Sea salt flakes and cracked black peppercorns, to savor
1½ tablespoons olive oil
⅓ turkey breasts, halved
1½ tablespoons rice vinegar
½ teaspoon marjoram

Per Serving: Calories 689; Fat 36.39g; Sodium 424mg; Carbs 2.74g; Fibre 0.1g; Sugar 1.34g; Protein 81.82g

Roasted Turkey Sausage with Cauliflower

⏱ **Prep: 45 minutes**   🍲 **Cook: 40 minutes**   📚 4

Preparation:

1. In a mixing bowl, thoroughly combine the turkey mince, garlic pepper, garlic powder, oregano, salt, and onion; stir well to combine.
2. Form the mixture into 4 sausages.
3. Cook the sausages in a frying pan over medium heat for 12 minutes or until they are no longer pink. Slice the sausages into 1/2-inch thick rounds.
4. Insert the crisper plate in the basket in zone 1; arrange the cauliflower florets onto the crisper plate, sprinkle them with thyme and basil, and spray them with pan spray, and then top them with the cooked turkey sausages.
5. Select ROAST mode, adjust the cooking temperature to 190°C and set the cooking time to 28 minutes.
6. Press the START/PAUSE button to begin cooking.
7. Toss the food halfway through cooking.
8. Serve warm and garnish with green onions if desired.

Ingredients:

455g turkey mince
1 teaspoon garlic pepper
1 teaspoon garlic powder
⅓ teaspoon dried oregano
½ teaspoon salt
55g onions, chopped
½ head cauliflower, broken into florets
⅓ teaspoon dried basil
½ teaspoon dried thyme, chopped

Per Serving: Calories 566; Fat 50.54g; Sodium 352mg; Carbs 4.26g; Fibre 1.1g; Sugar 1.63g; Protein 22.7g

Refreshing Apple Vinegar Chicken Breast

🕐 **Prep: 25 minutes**　🍲 **Cook: 30 minutes**　🍽 5

Preparation:

1. Mix the chicken breast with apple cider vinegar, dried basil, avocado oil, ground black pepper and salt to marinate the chicken breast for 20 minutes.
2. Install a crisper plate in both baskets, place the marinated chicken in the baskets, and insert the baskets into the unit.
3. Select Zone 1, select AIR FRY, set temperature to 190°C, and set time to 30 minutes. Select MATCH COOK to match Zone 2 settings to Zone 1. Press the START/PAUSE button to begin cooking.
4. When the cooking is complete, serve with vegetables on the side.

Ingredients:

900 g chicken breast, skinless, boneless
2 teaspoons dried basil
3 tablespoons apple cider vinegar
2 tablespoons avocado oil
1 teaspoon salt
1 teaspoon ground black pepper

Per Serving: Calories 251; Fat 8.59g; Sodium 558mg; Carbs 0.59g; Fibre 0.3g; Sugar 0.04g; Protein 40.4g

Chapter 4 Beef, Pork, and Lamb

39　Roasted Spiced Lamb Cutlets
39　Quick Peppermint Lamb Chops
40　Garlic Lamb Chops
40　Air Fried Marjoram Lamb Chops
41　Lamb Meatballs
41　Delicious Beef Bulgogi Burgers
42　Pork Patties with Blue Cheese
42　Fajita Meatball Lettuce Wraps
43　Cheese Black and Blue Burgers
43　Homemade Cheesy Mushroom Burgers
44　Dijon Chuck Eye Steak

Roasted Spiced Lamb Cutlets

Prep: 15 minutes   **Cook:** 50 minutes   **Serves:** 4

Preparation:

1. Chop the lamb cutlets roughly.
2. Coat the lamb cutlets with the remaining ingredients.
3. Insert the crisper plate in the basket in zone 1, and transfer the lamb cutlets to it.
4. Select AIR FRY mode, adjust the cooking temperature to 185°C and set the cooking time to 20 minutes.
5. Press the START/PAUSE button to begin cooking.
6. Serve warm and garnish with rosemary if desired.

Ingredients:

525g lamb cutlets
1 teaspoon white pepper
4 tablespoons avocado oil
1 teaspoon dried basil
1 tablespoon garlic powder
1 tablespoon ground coriander
1 tablespoon lemon zest, grated
3 tablespoons apple cider vinegar

Per Serving: Calories 514; Fat 39.08g; Sodium 115mg; Carbs 2.64g; Fibre 0.5g; Sugar 0.21g; Protein 37.02g

Quick Peppermint Lamb Chops

Prep: 10 minutes   **Cook:** 15 minutes   **Serves:** 4

Preparation:

1. Sprinkle the lamb chops with peppermint, avocado oil, and lemon juice.
2. Insert the crisper plate in the basket in zone 1, and transfer the lamb chops to it.
3. Select AIR FRY mode, adjust the cooking temperature to 205°C and set the cooking time to 12 minutes.
4. Press the START/PAUSE button to begin cooking.
5. Flip the lamb chops halfway through cooking.
6. Brush the sauce you like if desired and serve warm.

Ingredients:

455g lamb chops
1 teaspoon peppermint
1 teaspoon avocado oil
2 tablespoons lemon juice

Per Serving: Calories 363; Fat 31.34g; Sodium 64mg; Carbs 0.54g; Fibre 0g; Sugar 0.19g; Protein 18.54g

Garlic Lamb Chops

⏰ **Prep: 10 minutes** 🍲 **Cook: 20 minutes** 🍽 **4**

Preparation:

1. Sprinkle the lamb chops with garlic cloves and saffron.
2. Spray the lamb chops with cooking spray.
3. Insert the crisper plate in the basket in zone 1, and transfer the lamb chops to it.
4. Select AIR FRY mode, adjust the cooking temperature to 180°C and set the cooking time to 20 minutes.
5. Press the START/PAUSE button to begin cooking.
6. Flip the lamb chops halfway through cooking.
7. Serve warm with onion on the side.

Ingredients:

4 lamb chops
4 garlic cloves, minced
1 teaspoon saffron
Cooking spray

Per Serving: Calories 168; Fat 7.94g; Sodium 89mg; Carbs 1.11g; Fibre 0.1g; Sugar 0.03g; Protein 23.19g

Air Fried Marjoram Lamb Chops

⏰ **Prep: 10 minutes** 🍲 **Cook: 25 minutes** 🍽 **4**

Preparation:

1. In the shallow bowl, mix dried marjoram, salt, coconut cream, and coconut oil.
2. Carefully rub the lamb chops with marjoram mixture.
3. Insert the crisper plate in the basket in zone 1, and transfer the lamb chops to it.
4. Select AIR FRY mode, adjust the cooking temperature to 190°C and set the cooking time to 25 minutes.
5. Press the START/PAUSE button to begin cooking.
6. Serve warm with lemon if desired.

Ingredients:

900g lamb chops
1 teaspoon dried marjoram
1 teaspoon salt
1 tablespoon coconut cream
1 teaspoon coconut oil, melted

Per Serving: Calories 726; Fat 62.83g; Sodium 709mg; Carbs 0.34g; Fibre 0.1g; Sugar 0.01g; Protein 37.17g

Lamb Meatballs

⏰ **Prep: 15 minutes** 🍲 **Cook: 15 minutes** 📚 4

Preparation:

1. Mix minced lamb with flax meal, chili powder, and egg.
2. Make the balls from the lamb mixture.
3. Spray the balls with cooking spray.
4. Insert the crisper plate in the basket in zone 1, and transfer the meatballs to it.
5. Select AIR FRY mode, adjust the cooking temperature to 200°C and set the cooking time to 15 minutes.
6. Press the START/PAUSE button to begin cooking.
7. Serve warm.

Ingredients:

455g minced lamb
1 teaspoon flax meal
½ teaspoon chili powder
1 egg, beaten
Cooking spray

Per Serving: Calories 379; Fat 24.93g; Sodium 183mg; Carbs 0.73g; Fibre 0.1g; Sugar 0.25g; Protein 35.51g

Delicious Beef Bulgogi Burgers

⏰ **Prep: 20 minutes** 🍲 **Cook: 18 minutes** 📚 4

Preparation:

1. In a mixing bowl, thoroughly combine all ingredients until well combined.
2. Shape into four patties and spritz them with cooking oil on both sides.
3. Transfer the food to the basket in zone 1.
4. Select BAKE mode, adjust the cooking temperature to 180°C and set the cooking time to 18 minutes.
5. Press the START/PAUSE button to begin cooking.
6. Toss the food halfway through cooking.
7. Serve warm.

Ingredients:

675g beef mince
1 teaspoon garlic, minced
2 tablespoons spring onions, chopped
Sea salt and cracked black pepper, to taste
1 teaspoon Gochugaru (Korean chili powder)
½ teaspoon dried marjoram
1 teaspoon dried thyme
1 teaspoon mustard seeds
½ teaspoon shallot powder
½ teaspoon cumin powder
½ teaspoon paprika
1 tablespoon liquid smoke flavouring

Per Serving: Calories 235; Fat 10.05g; Sodium 747mg; Carbs 1.71g; Fibre 0.7g; Sugar 0.22g; Protein 35.13g

Pork Patties with Blue Cheese

⏰ Prep: 20 minutes   🍲 Cook: 45 minutes   📚 6

Preparation:

1. In a mixing dish, combine the pork, onion, garlic, tomato puree, and seasonings; mix to combine well.
2. Form the pork mixture into six patties.
3. Insert the crisper plates in the baskets. Divide the patties between the baskets in zone 1 and zone 2.
4. Select AIR FRY mode, adjust the cooking temperature to 195°C and set the cooking time to 41 minutes.
5. Press the MATCH COOK button and copy the zone 1 settings to zone 2.
6. Press the START/PAUSE button to begin cooking.
7. Flip the patties and adjust the temperature to 185°C after 23 minutes of cooking time.
8. Place the prepared burgers on a serving platter; serve warm with blue cheese.

Ingredients:

225g blue cheese, sliced
2 teaspoons dried basil
1 teaspoon smoked paprika
900g pork mince
2 tablespoons tomato puree
2 small-sized onions, peeled and chopped
½ teaspoon ground black pepper
3 garlic cloves, minced
1 teaspoon fine sea salt

Per Serving: Calories 545; Fat 37.98g; Sodium 759mg; Carbs 4.34g; Fibre 0.8g; Sugar 1.6g; Protein 44.28g

Fajita Meatball Lettuce Wraps

⏰ Prep: 10 minutes   🍲 Cook: 10 minutes   📚 4

Preparation:

1. Mix together all the ingredients in a large bowl until well combined.
2. Shape the meat mixture into eight 2.5 cm balls. Install a crisper plate in the Zone 1 basket. Spray a basket with avocado oil. Place the meatballs in the basket, leaving a little space between them.
3. Insert the basket into the unit. The unit will default to Zone
1. Select AIR FRY. Set the temperature to 175°C and set the time to 10 minutes. Press the START/PAUSE button to begin cooking until cooked through and no longer pink inside and the internal temperature reaches 75°C.
4. When the cooking is complete, serve each meatball on a lettuce leaf, topped with pico de gallo or salsa if desired. Serve with lime slices if desired.
5. Store the leftovers in an airtight container in the refrigerator for 3 days or in the freezer for up to a month. Before eating, cook for 4 minutes at 175°C in the air fryer, or until heated through.

Ingredients:

455 g minced beef (85% lean)
130 g salsa, plus more for serving if desired
30 g chopped onions
30 g diced green or red peppers
1 large egg, beaten
1 teaspoon fine sea salt
½ teaspoon chili powder
½ teaspoon ground cumin
1 clove garlic, minced
For Serving(optional):
8 leaves lettuce
Pico de gallo or salsa
Lime slices

Per Serving: Calories 282; Fat 13.97g; Sodium 1000mg; Carbs 5.97g; Fibre 1.4g; Sugar 2.63g; Protein 32.06g

Cheese Black and Blue Burgers

⏱ **Prep: 5 minutes**   🍳 **Cook: 10 minutes**   📚 2

Preparation:

1. Add the salt, pepper, and seasonings in a small bowl and combine well. Season the patties well on both sides with the seasoning mixture.
2. Install a crisper plate in the Zone 1 basket. Spray the basket with avocado oil. Place the patties in the basket, and insert the basket into the unit. The unit will default to Zone
1. Select AIR FRY. Set the temperature to 180°C and set the time to 7 minutes. Press the START/PAUSE button to begin cooking until the internal temperature reaching 65°C for a medium-done burger. Press the START/PAUSE button to turn off. Place the blue cheese over the patties and cook for additional 1 minute to melt the cheese.
3. When the cooking is complete, remove the burgers from the fryer and let rest for 5 minutes.
4. Slice the buns in half and smear 2 halves with a tablespoon of mayo each. Increase the heat to 205°C and place the buns in the fryer basket cut side up. Cook the buns for 1 to 2 minutes until golden brown.
5. When the cooking is complete, remove the buns from the fryer and place them on a serving plate. Place the burgers on the buns and top with 3 red onion slices and a lettuce leaf.
6. Best served fresh. Store the leftover patties in an airtight container in the refrigerator for 3 days or in the freezer for up to a month. Before eating, cook for 4 minutes at 175°C in the air fryer, or until heated through.

Ingredients:

½ teaspoon fine sea salt
¼ teaspoon ground black pepper
¼ teaspoon garlic powder
¼ teaspoon onion powder
¼ teaspoon smoked paprika
2 (115 g) hamburgers, 1.5 cm thick
50 g crumbled blue cheese (omit for dairy-free)
2 Hamburger Buns (here)
2 tablespoons mayonnaise
6 red onion slices
2 lettuce leaves

Per Serving: Calories 478; Fat 28.19g; Sodium 1608mg; Carbs 34.56g; Fibre 2.7g; Sugar 4.61g; Protein 21.61g

Homemade Cheesy Mushroom Burgers

⏱ **Prep: 5 minutes**   🍳 **Cook: 15 minutes**   📚 2

Preparation:

1. Clean the portobello mushrooms and remove the stems. Spray the mushrooms on all sides with avocado oil and season them with ½ teaspoon of the salt.
2. Install a crisper plate in the Zone 1 basket, place the mushrooms in the basket, and insert the basket into the unit. The unit will default to Zone 1. Select AIR FRY. Set the temperature to 180°C and set the time to 8 minutes. Press the START/PAUSE button to begin cooking until fork-tender and soft to the touch.
3. While cooking the mushroom, mix together the remaining ½ teaspoon of salt, pepper, onion powder, the paprika and garlic powder in a small bowl. Sprinkle the hamburger patties with the seasoning mixture.
4. When the mushrooms are done, transfer them from the fryer and place them on a serving plate with the cap side down.
5. Place the hamburger patties in the fryer and cook for 7 minutes or until the internal temperature reaches 65°C for a medium-done burger. Place a slice of Swiss cheese on each patty and cook for another minute to melt the cheese.
6. Place the burgers over the mushrooms. Drizzle with condiments and garnish with some vegetables if desired. Best served fresh.

Ingredients:

2 large portobello mushrooms
1 teaspoon fine sea salt, divided
¼ teaspoon garlic powder
¼ teaspoon ground black pepper
¼ teaspoon onion powder
¼ teaspoon smoked paprika
2 (115 g) hamburger patties, 1.5 cm thick
2 slices Swiss cheese (omit for dairy-free)
Condiments of choice, such as Ranch Dressing (here; use dairy-free if needed), prepared yellow mustard, or mayonnaise, for serving

Per Serving: Calories 291; Fat 20.01g; Sodium 1523mg; Carbs 11.49g; Fibre 1.3g; Sugar 0.97g; Protein 16.81g

Dijon Chuck Eye Steak

⏰ **Prep: 5 minutes**   🍲 **Cook: 12 minutes**   📚 4

Preparation:

1. Toss the steak with the remaining ingredients. Install a crisper plate in the both baskets, place the steak in the baskets, and insert the baskets into the unit.
2. Select Zone 1, select AIR FRY, set temperature to 205°C, and set time to 12 minutes. Select MATCH COOK to match Zone 2 settings to Zone 1. Press the START/PAUSE button to begin cooking. Press the START/PAUSE button to turn it over halfway through the cooking time.
3. When the cooking is complete, remove, sprinkle seasoning you live if desired, and serve. Bon appétit!

Ingredients:

675 g chuck eye steak
2 tablespoons olive oil
1 teaspoon paprika
1 tablespoon Dijon mustard
Salt and ground black pepper, to taste

Per Serving: Calories 311; Fat 17.89g; Sodium 169mg; Carbs 1.6g; Fibre 0.5g; Sugar 0.67g; Protein 36.65g

Chapter 5 Fish and Seafood

- 46 Fried Prawns Skewers
- 46 Flavourful Tuna Patties
- 47 Spicy Prawns and Cherry Tomato Kebabs
- 47 Crispy Fish Fillets
- 48 French Sea Bass with Sauce
- 48 Simple Salmon Patties
- 49 Baked Salmon Steaks with Butter and Wine
- 49 Roasted Lemony Prawns

Fried Prawns Skewers

⏰ **Prep:** 15 minutes   🍲 **Cook:** 5 minutes   📚 4

Preparation:

1. Add the prawns, vermouth, garlic, salt, black pepper, and olive oil in a ceramic bowl; let it sit for 1 hour in your refrigerator.
2. Discard the marinade and toss the prawns with flour. Thread the prawns on to skewers and transfer to the lightly greased cooking basket.
3. Insert the crisper plates in the baskets. Divide the skewers between the baskets in zone 1 and zone 2.
4. Select AIR FRY mode, adjust the cooking temperature to 205°C and set the cooking time to 5 minutes.
5. Press the MATCH COOK button and copy the zone 1 settings to zone 2.
6. Press the START/PAUSE button to begin cooking.
7. Flip the skewers halfway through cooking.
8. Serve warm.

Ingredients:

675g prawns
60ml vermouth
2 cloves garlic, crushed
Salt, to taste
¼ teaspoon black pepper, freshly ground
2 tablespoons olive oil
8 skewers, soaked in water for 30 minutes
1 lemon, cut into wedges

Per Serving: Calories 259; Fat 9.11g; Sodium 1521mg; Carbs 3.46g; Fibre 0.1g; Sugar 1.47g; Protein 34.92g

Flavourful Tuna Patties

⏰ **Prep:** 2 hours 20 minutes   🍲 **Cook:** 20 minutes   📚 4

Preparation:

1. In a mixing bowl, thoroughly combine the tuna, egg, garlic, shallots, Romano cheese, salt, and black pepper.
2. Shape the tuna mixture into four patties and place in your refrigerator for 2 hours.
3. Brush the patties with sesame oil on both sides.
4. Insert the crisper plate in the basket in zone 1, and transfer the tuna patties to it.
5. Select AIR FRY mode, adjust the cooking temperature to 180°C and set the cooking time to 14 minutes.
6. Press the START/PAUSE button to begin cooking.
7. Melt the butter in a pan over a moderate heat. Add the beer and whisk until it starts bubbling.
8. Stir in the grated cheese and cook for 3 to 4 minutes longer or until the cheese has melted.
9. Spoon the sauce over the fish patties and serve immediately.

Ingredients:

455g canned tuna, drained
1 egg, whisked
1 garlic clove, minced
2 tablespoons shallots, minced
100g Romano cheese, grated
Sea salt and ground black pepper, to taste
1 tablespoon sesame oil
Cheese Sauce:
1 tablespoon butter
240ml beer
2 tablespoons cheddar cheese, grated

Per Serving: Calories 457; Fat 30.85g; Sodium 834mg; Carbs 7.13g; Fibre 0.5g; Sugar 2.38g; Protein 37.99g

Spicy Prawns and Cherry Tomato Kebabs

⏱ **Prep: 25 minutes** 🍲 **Cook: 5 minutes** 🍽 4

Preparation:

1. Toss all ingredients in a mixing bowl until the prawns and tomatoes are covered on all sides.
2. Soak the wooden skewers in water for 15 minutes.
3. Thread the jumbo prawns and cherry tomatoes onto skewers.
4. Insert the crisper plates in the baskets. Divide the skewers between the baskets in zone 1 and zone 2.
5. Select AIR FRY mode, adjust the cooking temperature to 205°C and set the cooking time to 5 minutes.
6. Press the MATCH COOK button and copy the zone 1 settings to zone 2.
7. Press the START/PAUSE button to begin cooking.
8. Serve warm.

Ingredients:

675g jumbo prawns, cleaned, shelled and deveined
455g cherry tomatoes, halved
2 tablespoons butter, melted
1 tablespoons Sriracha sauce
Sea salt and ground black pepper, to taste
½ teaspoon dried oregano
½ teaspoon dried basil
1 teaspoon dried parsley flakes
½ teaspoon marjoram
½ teaspoon mustard seeds

Per Serving: Calories 268; Fat 17.81g; Sodium 1329mg; Carbs 29.34g; Fibre 7g; Sugar 15.32g; Protein 3.33g

Crispy Fish Fillets

⏱ **Prep: 25 minutes** 🍲 **Cook: 20 minutes** 🍽 4

Preparation:

1. Add the parmesan cheese, salt, peppercorns, fennel seeds, and tarragon to your food processor; blitz for about 20 seconds.
2. Drizzle fish fillets with dry white wine. Dump the egg into a shallow dish.
3. Coat the fish fillets with the beaten egg on all sides; then, coat them with the seasoned cracker mix.
4. Insert the crisper plates in the baskets. Divide the batter between the baskets in zone 1 and zone 2.
5. Select AIR FRY mode, adjust the cooking temperature to 175°C and set the cooking time to 17 minutes.
6. Press the MATCH COOK button and copy the zone 1 settings to zone 2.
7. Press the START/PAUSE button to begin cooking.
8. Serve warm.

Ingredients:

2 eggs, beaten
½ teaspoon tarragon
4 fish fillets, halved
2 tablespoons dry white wine
35g parmesan cheese, grated
1 teaspoon seasoned salt
⅓ teaspoon mixed peppercorns
½ teaspoon fennel seed

Per Serving: Calories 306; Fat 17.82g; Sodium 855mg; Carbs 6.53g; Fibre 0.2g; Sugar 0.36g; Protein 28.02g

French Sea Bass with Sauce

⏰ **Prep: 15 minutes**　🍲 **Cook: 10 minutes**　📚 2

Preparation:

1. Drizzle olive oil all over the fish fillets and transfer to the crisper plate in the basket.
2. Select AIR FRY mode, adjust the cooking temperature to 200°C and set the cooking time to 10 minutes.
3. Press the START/PAUSE button to begin cooking.
4. Flip the fish fillets halfway through cooking.
5. Make the sauce by whisking the remaining ingredients until everything is well incorporated. Place in the refrigerator until ready to serve.
6. When done, serve with vegetables on the side.

Ingredients:

1 tablespoon olive oil
2 sea bass fillets
Sauce:
120g mayonnaise
1 tablespoon capers, drained and chopped
1 tablespoon gherkins, drained and chopped
2 tablespoons spring onions, finely chopped
2 tablespoons lemon juice

Per Serving: Calories 330; Fat 20.95g; Sodium 296mg; Carbs 11.42g; Fibre 0.4g; Sugar 3.12g; Protein 24.24g

Simple Salmon Patties

⏰ **Prep: 15 minutes**　🍲 **Cook: 10 minutes**　📚 4

Preparation:

1. Mix the salmon, egg, garlic, green onions, and parmesan cheese in a bowl; knead with your hands until everything is well incorporated.
2. Shape the mixture into equally sized patties.
3. Insert the crisper plate in the basket in zone 1, and transfer the patties to it.
4. Select AIR FRY mode, adjust the cooking temperature to 190°C and set the cooking time to 10 minutes.
5. Press the START/PAUSE button to begin cooking.
6. Flip the patties halfway through cooking.
7. Whisk all of the sauce ingredients.
8. Serve the warm fish patties with the sauce on the side.

Ingredients:

455g salmon
1 egg
1 garlic clove, minced
2 green onions, minced
100g parmesan cheese
Sauce
1 teaspoon rice wine
1 ½ tablespoons soy sauce
A pinch of salt
1 teaspoon gochugaru (Korean red chili pepper flakes)

Per Serving: Calories 323; Fat 13.39g; Sodium 3993mg; Carbs 9.59g; Fibre 0.9g; Sugar 0.72g; Protein 40.6g

Baked Salmon Steaks with Butter and Wine

⏰ Prep: 45 minutes   🍲 Cook: 10 minutes   📚 4

Preparation:

1. Place all ingredients in a large ceramic dish. Cover the dish and let the food marinate for 30 minutes in the refrigerator.
2. Insert the crisper plates in the baskets.
3. Divide the salmon steaks between the baskets in zone 1 and zone 2.
4. Select BAKE mode, adjust the cooking temperature to 200°C and set the cooking time to 10 minutes.
5. Press the MATCH COOK button and copy the zone 1 settings to zone 2.
6. Press the START/PAUSE button to begin cooking.
7. Flip the salmon steaks and baste them with the reserved marinade halfway through cooking.
8. When done, the salmon steaks should be easily flaked with fork.
9. Serve warm with some vegetables on the side.

Ingredients:

2 cloves garlic, minced
4 tablespoons butter, melted
Sea salt and ground black pepper, to taste
1 teaspoon smoked paprika
½ teaspoon onion powder
1 tablespoon lime juice
60ml dry white wine
4 salmon steaks

Per Serving: Calories 283; Fat 19.75g; Sodium 785mg; Carbs 1.73g; Fibre 0.4g; Sugar 0.33g; Protein 23.85g

Roasted Lemony Prawns

⏰ Prep: 10 minutes   🍲 Cook: 10 minutes   📚 4

Preparation:

1. In a bowl, thoroughly combine all the ingredients, coating the prawns on all sides.
2. Insert the crisper plate in the basket in zone 1, and transfer the prawns to it.
3. Select ROAST mode, adjust the cooking temperature to 195°C and set the cooking time to 8 minutes.
4. Press the START/PAUSE button to begin cooking.
5. Serve warm.

Ingredients:

1 teaspoon crushed red pepper flakes, or more to taste
2 cloves garlic, finely minced
Garlic pepper, to savor
1½ tablespoons fresh parsley, roughly chopped
455g prawns, deveined
1 ½ tablespoons lemon juice
4 tablespoons olive oil
Sea salt flakes, to taste

Per Serving: Calories 255; Fat 14.14g; Sodium 428mg; Carbs 2.09g; Fibre 0.3g; Sugar 0.78g; Protein 2.09g

Chapter 6 Snacks and Starters

- 51 Cheese Broccoli Tots
- 51 Healthy Broccoli Hash Brown
- 52 Easy Aubergine Bites
- 52 Creamy Broccoli Puree
- 53 Roasted Brussels Sprouts
- 53 Crispy Red Beetroot Chips
- 54 Honeyed Chicken Wings
- 54 Quick Tortilla Chips
- 55 Simple Cheese-Stuffed Mushrooms
- 55 Spicy Juicy Chicken Drumsticks
- 56 Sweet-and-Spicy Spare Ribs

Cheese Broccoli Tots

⏰ **Prep: 15 minutes** 🍲 **Cook: 8 minutes** 📚 4

Preparation:

1. In the mixing bowl, mix mascarpone with Cheddar cheese, broccoli, and onion powder.
2. Make the broccoli tots from the mixture and transfer them to the crisper plates in the baskets.
3. Sprinkle the broccoli tots with avocado oil.
4. Select BAKE mode, adjust the cooking temperature to 205°C and set the cooking time to 8 minutes.
5. Press the MATCH COOK button and copy the zone 1 settings to zone 2.
6. Press the START/PAUSE button to begin cooking.

Ingredients:

1 teaspoon mascarpone
125g Cheddar cheese, shredded
270g broccoli, chopped, boiled
¼ teaspoon onion powder
1 teaspoon avocado oil

Per Serving: Calories 79; Fat 4.42g; Sodium 401mg; Carbs 4.77g; Fibre 0.8g; Sugar 2.63g; Protein 5.72g

Healthy Broccoli Hash Brown

⏰ **Prep: 5 minutes** 🍲 **Cook: 15 minutes** 📚 4

Preparation:

1. Mix broccoli with eggs and transfer the mixture to the basket in zone 1.
2. Add coconut oil and dried oregano.
3. ROAST the meal at 205°C for 15 minutes. Stir the meal every 5 minutes.
4. Serve warm.

Ingredients:

180g broccoli, chopped
3 eggs, whisked
1 tablespoon coconut oil
1 teaspoon dried oregano

Per Serving: Calories 131; Fat 10.74g; Sodium 83mg; Carbs 1.5g; Fibre 0.6g; Sugar 0.57g; Protein 7.38g

Easy Aubergine Bites

⏱ **Prep: 10 minutes**   🍲 **Cook: 10 minutes**   📚 5

Preparation:

1. Grease the crisper plates in the baskets with coconut oil.
2. Arrange the sliced aubergines onto the crisper plates in one layer.
3. Top them with Parmesan.
4. Select AIR FRY mode, adjust the cooking temperature to 200°C and set the cooking time to 10 minutes.
5. Press the MATCH COOK button and copy the zone 1 settings to zone 2.
6. Press the START/PAUSE button to begin cooking.
7. When done, serve and sprinkle something for garnishing if desired.

Ingredients:

2 medium aubergines, trimmed, sliced
100g Parmesan, grated
1 teaspoon coconut oil, melted

Per Serving: Calories 146; Fat 2.43g; Sodium 265mg; Carbs 21.96g; Fibre 6.6g; Sugar 8.08g; Protein 11.22g

Creamy Broccoli Puree

⏱ **Prep: 10 minutes**   🍲 **Cook: 20 minutes**   📚 4

Preparation:

1. Put coconut oil in the basket.
2. Add broccoli, heavy cream, and salt.
3. ROAST the food at 185°C for 20 minutes.
4. Mash the cooked broccoli mixture until you get the soft puree.

Ingredients:

455g broccoli, chopped
1 tablespoon coconut oil
60g heavy cream
1 teaspoon salt

Per Serving: Calories 80; Fat 6.73g; Sodium 622mg; Carbs 3.44g; Fibre 3.1g; Sugar 0.64g; Protein 3.75g

52 | Chapter 6 Snacks and Starters

Roasted Brussels Sprouts

⏰ **Prep: 10 minutes**   🍲 **Cook: 15 minutes**   📚 6

Preparation:

1. Put coconut oil in the baskets.
2. Divide Brussels sprouts, garlic powder, ground coriander, and apple cider vinegar between the baskets.
3. Select ROAST mode, adjust the cooking temperature to 200°C and set the cooking time to 13 minutes.
4. Press the MATCH COOK button and copy the zone 1 settings to zone 2.
5. Press the START/PAUSE button to begin cooking.
6. Toss the food from time to time during cooking.

Ingredients:

455g Brussels sprouts
1 teaspoon garlic powder
1 teaspoon ground coriander
1 tablespoon coconut oil
1 tablespoon apple cider vinegar

Per Serving: Calories 54; Fat 2.5g; Sodium 19mg; Carbs 7.17g; Fibre 2.9g; Sugar 1.69g; Protein 2.64g

Crispy Red Beetroot Chips

⏰ **Prep: 15 minutes**   🍲 **Cook: 30 minutes**   📚 4

Preparation:

1. Install a crisper plate in the Zone 1 basket.
2. Toss the beetroot with the remaining ingredients in a mixing bowl and transfer to the air fryer basket. Then insert the basket in the unit.
3. Select Zone 1, select AIR FRY, set the temperature to 165°C, and set the time for 30 minutes. Press START/PAUSE to begin cooking.
4. Turn them over halfway through the cooking time. Enjoy!

Ingredients:

455 g red beetroot, peeled and cut into ½ cm slices
1 tablespoon olive oil
1 teaspoon cayenne pepper
Sea salt and ground black pepper, to taste

Per Serving: Calories 85; Fat 3.67g; Sodium 89mg; Carbs 12.16g; Fibre 3.5g; Sugar 8.29g; Protein 2.1g

Honeyed Chicken Wings

⏰ **Prep: 15 minutes** 🍲 **Cook: 18 minutes** 🍽 **4**

Preparation:

1. Toss the chicken wings with the remaining ingredients in a mixing bowl.
2. Install a crisper plate in both baskets. Place the seasoned chicken wings in the basket and insert in the unit.
3. Select Zone 1, select AIR FRY, set the temperature to 195°C, and set time to 18 minutes. Select MATCH COOK to match Zone 2 settings to Zone
1. Press the START/PAUSE button to begin cooking.
4. Turn them over halfway through the cooking time.
5. When done, serve with sauce you like and vegetables on the side if desired. Bon appétit!

Ingredients:

900 g chicken wings
55 g honey
2 tablespoons fish sauce
2 garlic cloves, crushed
1 teaspoon ginger, peeled and grated
2 tablespoons butter, melted
Sea salt and ground black pepper, to taste

Per Serving: Calories 411; Fat 13.82g; Sodium 938mg; Carbs 19.45g; Fibre 0.3g; Sugar 18.34g; Protein 50.74g

Quick Tortilla Chips

⏰ **Prep: 5 minutes** 🍲 **Cook: 3 minutes** 🍽 **2**

Preparation:

1. Slice the corn tortillas into triangles and lightly brush with olive oil.
2. Install a crisper plate in the Zone 1 basket. Place the tortilla pieces in the basket and insert in the unit.
3. Select Zone 1, select AIR FRY, set the temperature to 200°C, and set the time for 3 minutes. Press START/PAUSE to begin cooking.
4. Season with salt before serving.

Ingredients:

8 corn tortillas
Salt to taste
1 tbsp. olive oil

Per Serving: Calories 269; Fat 9.49g; Sodium 625mg; Carbs 42.85g; Fibre 6g; Sugar 0.84g; Protein 5.47g

Simple Cheese-Stuffed Mushrooms

⏰ **Prep: 10 minutes**   🍲 **Cook: 7 minutes**   📚 **4**

Preparation:

1. Install a crisper plate in the Zone 1 basket.
2. Mix together the butter, cheese, chives, salt, garlic, cayenne pepper, and black pepper in a bowl.
3. Divide the filling between the mushrooms and place the mushrooms in the Air Fryer basket.
4. Select Zone 1, select AIR FRY, set the temperature to 205°C, and set the time for 7 minutes. Press START/PAUSE to begin cooking.
5. Flip halfway through the cooking time. Serve and garnish with fresh dill.

Ingredients:

1 tablespoon butter
150 g Pecorino Romano cheese, grated
2 tablespoons chives, chopped
1 tablespoon minced garlic
½ teaspoon cayenne pepper
Sea salt and ground black pepper, to taste
455 g button mushrooms, stems removed

Per Serving: Calories 535; Fat 15.54g; Sodium 648mg; Carbs 88.97g; Fibre 13.4g; Sugar 3.46g; Protein 24.85g

Spicy Juicy Chicken Drumsticks

⏰ **Prep: 10 minutes**   🍲 **Cook: 18 minutes**   📚 **5**

Preparation:

1. Place the chicken drumsticks in a large bowl and toss with the remaining ingredients.
2. Install a crisper plate in the Zone 1 basket. Place the chicken drumettes in the basket and insert the basket into the unit.
3. Select Zone 1, select AIR FRY, set the temperature to 195°C, and set the time for 18 minutes. Press START/PAUSE to begin cooking. Flip halfway through the cooking time.
4. Once done, serve hot.

Ingredients:

900 g chicken drumsticks
1 teaspoon ancho chile pepper
1 teaspoon smoked paprika
1 teaspoon onion powder
1 teaspoon garlic powder
Salt and ground black pepper, to taste
¼ tsp black pepper
2 tablespoons olive oil

Per Serving: Calories 268; Fat 10.67g; Sodium 139mg; Carbs 3.77g; Fibre 1.2g; Sugar 0.55g; Protein 37.7g

Sweet-and-Spicy Spare Ribs

Prep: 6 minutes **Cook: 35 minutes** **4**

Preparation:

1. Install a crisper plate in the Zone 1 basket and lightly grease with cooking oil.
2. Toss all the ingredients in a bowl and transfer to the air fryer basket. Then insert the basket into the unit.
3. Select Zone 1, select AIR FRY, set the temperature to 175°C, and set the time for 35 minutes. Press START/PAUSE to begin cooking.
4. Flip halfway through the cooking time.
5. Once done, serve hot.

Ingredients:

675 g spare ribs
Salt and ground black pepper, to taste
2 teaspoons brown sugar
1 teaspoon paprika
1 teaspoon chile powder
1 teaspoon garlic powder

Per Serving: Calories 254; Fat 9.7g; Sodium 116mg; Carbs 3.66g; Fibre 0.5g; Sugar 1.91g; Protein 35.81g

Chapter 7 Desserts

58	Chocolate Cookies
58	Easy Popcorn Chicken Balls
59	Yummy Chocolate Brownies
59	Flavourful Fluffy Chocolate Cake
60	Sweet Espresso Brownies
60	Basic Vanilla Cupcakes
61	Homemade Double Chocolate Brownies
61	Soft Blueberry Cupcakes
62	Crispy Chocolate Chips Cookies
62	Simple Spanish Churros
63	Fresh Blackberry Muffins
63	Tasty Chocolate Lava Cake
64	Delicious Chocolate Mascarpone Cake

Chocolate Cookies

⏱ **Prep:** 20 minutes   🍲 **Cook:** 15 minutes   📚 10

Preparation:

1. In a mixing bowl, thoroughly combine the flour, sweetener, and butter. Mix until your mixture resembles breadcrumbs.
2. Gradually, add the egg and vanilla essence. Shape the dough into small balls.
3. Insert the crisper plates in the baskets. Line the crisper plates with parchment paper and divide the food between the baskets in zone 1 and zone 2.
4. Select BAKE mode, adjust the cooking temperature to 175°C and set the cooking time to 15 minutes.
5. Press the MATCH COOK button and copy the zone 1 settings to zone 2.
6. Press the START/PAUSE button to begin cooking.
7. Flip the food after 10 minutes of cooking time.
8. Transfer the freshly baked cookies to a cooling rack.
9. Melt the double cream and bakers' chocolate in the oven at 175°C, then add the cardamom seeds and stir them well.
10. Spread the filling over the cooled biscuits and sandwich together.

Ingredients:

200g almond flour
60g coconut flour
100g sweetener
125g butter, softened
1 egg, beaten
1 teaspoon vanilla essence
100g double cream
75g cooking chocolate, unsweetened
1 teaspoon cardamom seeds, finely crushed

Per Serving: Calories 166; Fat 14.91g; Sodium 125mg; Carbs 6.75g; Fibre 0.4g; Sugar 5.09g; Protein 1.66g

Easy Popcorn Chicken Balls

⏱ **Prep:** 10 minutes   🍲 **Cook:** 12 minutes   📚 6

Preparation:

1. Mix the chicken mince with Italian seasonings, egg, and coconut flour.
2. Make the small balls from the chicken mixture. Sprinkle the popcorn balls with avocado oil.
3. Insert the crisper plates in the baskets. Divide the balls between the baskets in zone 1 and zone 2.
4. Select AIR FRY mode, adjust the cooking temperature to 185°C and set the cooking time to 12 minutes.
5. Press the MATCH COOK button and copy the zone 1 settings to zone 2.
6. Press the START/PAUSE button to begin cooking.
7. Flip the food halfway through cooking.
8. When done, serve with sauce you like.

Ingredients:

280g chicken mince
1 teaspoon Italian seasonings
1 egg, beaten
30g coconut flour
1 tablespoon avocado oil

Per Serving: Calories 208; Fat 15.35g; Sodium 115mg; Carbs 0.82g; Fibre 0.2g; Sugar 0.42g; Protein 15.65g

Yummy Chocolate Brownies

⏰ **Prep: 30 minutes** 🍲 **Cook: 22 minutes** 📚 **8**

Preparation:

1. Spritz the sides and bottom of a baking pan with cooking spray.
2. In a mixing dish, beat the melted butter with sweetener until fluffy. Fold in the eggs and beat again.
3. Add the vanilla, flour, baking powder, cocoa, salt, and ground cardamom. Mix them until everything is well combined.
4. Transfer them to the baking pan and then place the pan in the basket in zone 1.
5. Select BAKE mode, adjust the cooking temperature to 175°C and set the cooking time to 22 minutes.
6. Press the START/PAUSE button to begin cooking.
7. Enjoy!

Ingredients:

115g butter, melted
30g sweetener
2 eggs
1 teaspoon vanilla essence
2 tablespoons flaxseed meal
120g coconut flour
1 teaspoon baking powder
50g cocoa powder, unsweetened
A pinch of salt
A pinch of ground cardamom

Per Serving: Calories 168; Fat 15.74g; Sodium 170mg; Carbs 5.78g; Fibre 2.7g; Sugar 1.16g; Protein 4.05g

Flavourful Fluffy Chocolate Cake

⏰ **Prep: 20 minutes** 🍲 **Cook: 15 minutes** 📚 **6**

Preparation:

1. Melt the butter, chocolate, and stevia in a saucepan over medium heat.
2. Add the other ingredients to the cooled chocolate mixture; stir to combine well.
3. Scrape the batter into a lightly greased baking pan.
4. Transfer the pan to the basket in zone 1.
5. Select BAKE mode, adjust the cooking temperature to 165°C and set the cooking time to 15 minutes.
6. Press the START/PAUSE button to begin cooking.
7. When done, the centre should be springy and a toothpick comes out dry. Enjoy!

Ingredients:

60g butter, at room temperature
85g chocolate, unsweetened and chopped
1 tablespoon liquid stevia
180g coconut flour
A pinch of fine sea salt
2 eggs, whisked
½ teaspoon vanilla extract

Per Serving: Calories 133; Fat 4.35g; Sodium 146mg; Carbs 18.95g; Fibre 1.3g; Sugar 14.24g; Protein 4.03g

Sweet Espresso Brownies

⏱ **Prep: 40 minutes** 🍲 **Cook: 35 minutes** 📚 **8**

Preparation:

1. Microwave the chocolate and almond butter until completely melted; allow the mixture to cool at room temperature.
2. Whisk the eggs, sweetener, cinnamon, espresso powder, coffee extract, ancho chili powder, and lime zest.
3. Add the vanilla mixture to the chocolate/butter mixture. Stir in the almond meal and coconut flour along with baking soda, baking powder and cocoa powder.
4. Press the batter into a lightly buttered cake pan.
5. Transfer the pan to the basket in zone 1.
6. Select BAKE mode, adjust the cooking temperature to 175°C and set the cooking time to 35 minutes.
7. Press the START/PAUSE button to begin cooking.
8. In the meantime, beat the butter and mascarpone cheese until creamy. Add in the melted chocolate chips and vanilla paste.
9. Gradually stir in the powdered sweetener and salt; beat until everything's well combined.
10. Lastly, frost the brownies and serve.

Ingredients:

125g unsweetened chocolate, chopped into chunks
2 tablespoons instant espresso powder
1 tablespoon cocoa powder, unsweetened
125g almond butter
50g almond meal
20g sweetener
1 teaspoon pure coffee extract
½ teaspoon lime peel zest
30g coconut flour
2 eggs plus 1 egg yolk
½ teaspoon baking soda
½ teaspoon baking powder
½ teaspoon ground cinnamon
⅓ teaspoon ancho chili powder

For the Chocolate Mascarpone Frosting:
100g mascarpone cheese, at room temperature
25g unsweetened chocolate chips
50g powdered sweetener
55g unsalted butter, at room temperature
1 teaspoon vanilla paste
A pinch of fine sea salt

Per Serving: Calories 439; Fat 27.51g; Sodium 424mg; Carbs 41.99g; Fibre 2.6g; Sugar 34.17g; Protein 8.07g

Basic Vanilla Cupcakes

⏱ **Prep: 30 minutes** 🍲 **Cook: 15 minutes** 📚 **4**

Preparation:

1. Mix the flour, coconut milk, eggs, coconut oil, vanilla, and cardamom in a large bowl.
2. Let the mixture stand for 20 minutes.
3. Spoon the batter into two greased muffin tins.
4. Transfer the muffin tins to the baskets in zone 1 and zone 2.
5. Select BAKE mode, adjust the cooking temperature to 110°C and set the cooking time to 5 minutes.
6. Press the MATCH COOK button and copy the zone 1 settings to zone 2.
7. Press the START/PAUSE button to begin cooking.
8. Decorate the cupcakes with coconut chips and enjoy.

Ingredients:

60g coconut flour
80ml coconut milk
2 eggs
1 tablespoon coconut oil, melted
1 teaspoon vanilla
A pinch of ground cardamom

Per Serving: Calories 151; Fat 13.07g; Sodium 86mg; Carbs 3.27g; Fibre 0.9g; Sugar 1.94g; Protein 5.21g

Homemade Double Chocolate Brownies

⏰ **Prep: 55 minutes**   🍲 **Cook: 20 minutes**   📚 10

Preparation:

1. Microwave white chocolate and coconut oil until everything's melted; allow the mixture to cool at room temperature.
2. Thoroughly whisk the eggs, monk fruit, rum extract, cocoa powder and cardamom.
3. Add the rum mixture to the chocolate mixture. Stir in the flour and coconut flakes; mix them to combine.
4. Mix cranberries with whiskey and let them soak for 15 minutes. Fold them into the batter. Press the batter into a lightly buttered cake pan.
5. Transfer the pan to the basket in zone 1.
6. Select BAKE mode, adjust the cooking temperature to 170°C and set the cooking time to 35 minutes.
7. Allow them to cool slightly on a wire rack before slicing and serving.

Ingredients:

3 tablespoons whiskey
200g white chocolate
75g almond flour
25g coconut flakes
120ml coconut oil
2 eggs plus an egg yolk, whisked
150g monk fruit
2 tablespoons cocoa powder, unsweetened
¼ teaspoon ground cardamom
1 teaspoon pure rum extract

Per Serving: Calories 201; Fat 11.3g; Sodium 36mg; Carbs 23.5g; Fibre 1.2g; Sugar 13.85g; Protein 2.58g

Soft Blueberry Cupcakes

⏰ **Prep: 20 minutes**   🍲 **Cook: 15 minutes**   📚 6

Preparation:

1. In the first bowl, thoroughly combine the erythritol, almond flour, baking soda, and baking powder, salt, nutmeg, cinnamon and cocoa powder.
2. In the second bowl, cream the butter, egg, rum extract, and milk; whisk them to combine well.
3. Add the wet mixture to the dry mixture. Fold in blueberries.
4. Press the prepared batter mixture into a lightly greased muffin tin.
5. Insert the crisper plates in the baskets. Divide the muffin tins between the baskets in zone 1 and zone 2.
6. Select BAKE mode, adjust the cooking temperature to 175°C and set the cooking time to 15 minutes.
7. Press the MATCH COOK button and copy the zone 1 settings to zone 2.
8. Press the START/PAUSE button to begin cooking.
9. Use a toothpick to check.
10. Serve warm.

Ingredients:

3 teaspoons cocoa powder, unsweetened
95g blueberries
125g almond flour
120ml milk
115g butter, room temperature
3 eggs
150g granulated erythritol
1 teaspoon pure rum extract
½ teaspoon baking soda
1 teaspoon baking powder
¼ teaspoon grated nutmeg
½ teaspoon ground cinnamon
⅛ teaspoon salt

Per Serving: Calories 335; Fat 21.12g; Sodium 339mg; Carbs 32.47g; Fibre 0.8g; Sugar 30.8g; Protein 5.65g

Chapter 7 Desserts | 61

Crispy Chocolate Chips Cookies

⏰ Prep: 20 minutes   🍲 Cook: 15 minutes   ≋ 8

Preparation:

1. In a mixing dish, beat the butter and sweetener until creamy and uniform. Stir in the peanut butter and vanilla.
2. In another mixing dish, thoroughly combine the flour, cocoa powder, baking powder, cinnamon, and crystallized ginger.
3. Add the flour mixture to the peanut butter mixture; mix to combine well. Afterwards, fold in the chocolate chips.
4. Insert the crisper plates in the baskets and line them with parchment paper.
5. Divide the food between the baskets in zone 1 and zone 2.
6. Select BAKE mode, adjust the cooking temperature to 185°C and set the cooking time to 11 minutes.
7. Press the MATCH COOK button and copy the zone 1 settings to zone 2.
8. Press the START/PAUSE button to begin cooking.
9. Bon appétit!

Ingredients:

115g butter, at room temperature
40g sweetener
65g chunky peanut butter
1 teaspoon vanilla paste
100g almond flour
80g coconut flour
35g cocoa powder, unsweetened
1 ½ teaspoons baking powder
¼ teaspoon ground cinnamon
¼ teaspoon crystallized ginger
85g chocolate chips, unsweetened

Per Serving: Calories 302; Fat 18.02g; Sodium 152mg; Carbs 30.96g; Fibre 3.1g; Sugar 9.14g; Protein 4.76g

Simple Spanish Churros

⏰ Prep: 20 minutes   🍲 Cook: 10 minutes   ≋ 4

Preparation:

1. Boil the water in a pan over medium-high heat; now, add the sweetener, salt, nutmeg, and cloves; cook them until dissolved.
2. Add the butter and turn the heat to low. Gradually stir in the almond flour, whisking continuously, until the mixture forms a ball.
3. Turn off the heat; fold in the eggs one at a time, stirring them to combine well.
4. Pour the mixture into a piping bag with a large star tip.
5. Squeeze 10 cm strips of dough into a suitable baking pan.
6. Transfer the pan to the basket in zone 1.
7. Select BAKE mode, adjust the cooking temperature to 210°C and set the cooking time to 6 minutes.
8. Press the START/PAUSE button to begin cooking.
9. Serve and enjoy.

Ingredients:

180ml water
1 tablespoon sweetener
¼ teaspoon sea salt
¼ teaspoon grated nutmeg
¼ teaspoon ground cloves
6 tablespoons butter
75g almond flour
2 eggs

Per Serving: Calories 220; Fat 22.26g; Sodium 334mg; Carbs 0.64g; Fibre 0.1g; Sugar 0.35g; Protein 4.72g

Fresh Blackberry Muffins

⏱ **Prep: 20 minutes** 🍲 **Cook: 15 minutes** 📚 **8**

Preparation:

1. In a mixing bowl, combine the almond flour, baking soda, baking powder, sweetener, and salt. Whisk to combine well.
2. In another mixing bowl, mix the milk, eggs, coconut oil, and vanilla.
3. Add the wet egg mixture to dry the flour mixture. Then, carefully fold in the fresh blackberries; gently stir to combine.
4. Scrape the batter mixture into the muffin cups.
5. Insert the crisper plates in the baskets. Divide the muffin cups between the baskets in zone 1 and zone 2.
6. Select BAKE mode, adjust the cooking temperature to 175°C and set the cooking time to 12 minutes.
7. Press the MATCH COOK button and copy the zone 1 settings to zone 2.
8. Press the START/PAUSE button to begin cooking. Flip the food halfway through cooking.
9. Sprinkle some extra icing sugar over the top of each muffin if desired. Serve and enjoy!

Ingredients:

150g almond flour
½ teaspoon baking soda
1 teaspoon baking powder
¼ teaspoon salt
15g sweetener
2 eggs, whisked
120ml milk
60ml coconut oil, melted
½ teaspoon vanilla paste
75g fresh blackberries

Per Serving: Calories 161; Fat 7.8g; Sodium 175mg; Carbs 19.03g; Fibre 0.8g; Sugar 4.01g; Protein 3.94g

Tasty Chocolate Lava Cake

⏱ **Prep: 15 minutes** 🍲 **Cook: 10 minutes** 📚 **4**

Preparation:

1. Spritz the sides and bottom of a baking pan that fits the air fryer basket with nonstick cooking spray.
2. Microwave the butter and dark chocolate in a microwave-safe bowl until melted. Whisk the eggs and monk fruit in a medium bowl and mix until frothy.
3. Add the chocolate mixture into the egg mixture and stir in the almond meal, cinnamon, baking powder, and star anise. Mix until everything is well combined.
4. Arrange the batter onto the prepared pan. Place the pan in the Zone 1 basket and insert the basket in the unit.
5. Select Zone 1, select BAKE, set the temperature to 190°C, and set time for 10 minutes. Press START/PAUSE to begin cooking.
6. When cooking is complete, let rest for 2 minutes. Invert on a plate while warm and serve. Bon appétit!

Ingredients:

100 g butter, melted
100 g dark chocolate
2 eggs, lightly whisked
2 tablespoons monk fruit sweetener
2 tablespoons almond meal
1 teaspoon baking powder
½ teaspoon ground cinnamon
¼ teaspoon ground star anise

Per Serving: Calories 451; Fat 40.34g; Sodium 245mg; Carbs 16g; Fibre 3.4g; Sugar 7.4g; Protein 7.47g

Delicious Chocolate Mascarpone Cake

⏰ **Prep: 15 minutes** 🍲 **Cook: 18 minutes** 📚 6

Preparation:

1. In a bowl, mix together the stevia, coconut flour, and butter. Press the mixture into the bottom of a lightly greased baking pan that fits the air fryer basket. Place the pan in the Zone 1 basket and insert the basket in the unit.
2. Select Zone 1, select BAKE, set the temperature to 180°C, and set time for 18 minutes. Press START/PAUSE to begin cooking.
3. Once done, transfer it to your freezer for 20 minutes.
4. Meanwhile, mix up the remaining ingredients to make the cheesecake topping. Place this topping over the crust and let it to cool in your freezer for 15 more minutes. Serve well chilled with ice cream if desired.

Ingredients:

2 tablespoons stevia
55 g coconut flour
110 g butter
120 g mascarpone cheese, at room temperature
100 g baker's chocolate, unsweetened
1 teaspoon vanilla extract
2 drops peppermint extract

Per Serving: Calories 290; Fat 22.26g; Sodium 294mg; Carbs 16.91g; Fibre 0.7g; Sugar 13.4g; Protein 6.12g

Conclusion

Cooking is an art, and the Ninja Foodi Dual Zone Air Fryer has even made everything better and smoother. If you were planning to acquire a Ninja Foodi Dual Zone Air Fryer, that is the best option you will ever think of. You will enjoy the many benefits described in this guide when using this appliance.

Still, if you are a beginner, this guide is all you need. Learn the basics of the Ninja Foodi Dual Zone Air Fryer, then try the many recipes we've provided in this guide. With time, you will become a pro in making meals using this powerful kitchen appliance from Ninja. Don't forget to get extra creative when preparing meals to make the meals aromatic and colorful for a fulfilling experience.

Appendix 1 Measurement Conversion Chart

VOLUME EQUIVALENTS (LIQUID)

US STANDARD	US STANDARD (OUNCES)	METRIC (APPROXIMATE)
2 tablespoons	1 fl.oz	30 mL
¼ cup	2 fl.oz	60 mL
½ cup	4 fl.oz	120 mL
1 cup	8 fl.oz	240 mL
1½ cup	12 fl.oz	355 mL
2 cups or 1 pint	16 fl.oz	475 mL
4 cups or 1 quart	32 fl.oz	1 L
1 gallon	128 fl.oz	4 L

TEMPERATURES EQUIVALENTS

FAHRENHEIT (F)	CELSIUS (C) (APPROXIMATE)
225 °F	107 °C
250 °F	120 °C
275 °F	135 °C
300 °F	150 °C
325 °F	160 °C
350 °F	180 °C
375 °F	190 °C
400 °F	205 °C
425 °F	220 °C
450 °F	235 °C
475 °F	245 °C
500 °F	260 °C

VOLUME EQUIVALENTS (DRY)

US STANDARD	METRIC (APPROXIMATE)
⅛ teaspoon	0.5 mL
¼ teaspoon	1 mL
½ teaspoon	2 mL
¾ teaspoon	4 mL
1 teaspoon	5 mL
1 tablespoon	15 mL
¼ cup	59 mL
½ cup	118 mL
¾ cup	177 mL
1 cup	235 mL
2 cups	475 mL
3 cups	700 mL
4 cups	1 L

WEIGHT EQUIVALENTS

US STANDARD	METRIC (APPROXIMATE)
1 ounce	28 g
2 ounces	57 g
5 ounces	142 g
10 ounces	284 g
15 ounces	425 g
16 ounces (1 pound)	455 g
1.5 pounds	680 g
2 pounds	907 g

Appendix 2 Air Fryer Cooking Chart

vegetables	Temp (°F)	Time (min)
Asparagus (1-inch slices)	400	5
Beets (sliced)	350	25
Beets (whole)	400	40
Bell Peppers (sliced)	350	13
Broccoli	400	6
Brussels Sprouts (halved)	380	15
Carrots(½-inch slices)	380	15
Cauliflower (florets)	400	12
Eggplant (1½-inch cubes)	400	15
Fennel (quartered)	370	15
Mushrooms (¼-inch slices)	400	5
Onion (pearl)	400	10
Parsnips (½-inch chunks)	380	5
Peppers (1-inch chunks)	400	15
Potatoes (baked, whole)	400	40
Squash (½-inch chunks)	400	12
Tomatoes (cherry)	400	4
Zucchni (½-inch sticks)	400	12

Meat	Temp (°F)	Time (min)
Bacon	400	5 to 7
Beef Eye Round Roast (4 lbs.)	390	50 to 60
Burger (4 oz.)	370	16 to 20
Chicken Breasts, bone-in (1.25 lbs.)	370	25
Chicken Breasts, boneless (4 oz.)	380	12
Chicken Drumsticks (2.5 lbs.)	370	20
Chicken Thighs, bone-in (2 lbs.)	380	22
Chicken Thighs, boneless (1.5 lbs.)	380	18 to 20
Chicken Legs, bone-in (1.75 lbs.)	380	30
Chicken Wings (2 lbs.)	400	12
Flank Steak (1.5 lbs.)	400	12
Game Hen (halved, 2 lbs.)	390	20
Loin (2 lbs.)	360	55
London Broil (2 lbs.)	400	20 to 28
Meatballs (3-inch)	380	10
Rack of Lamb (1.5-2 lbs.)	380	22
Sausages	380	15
Whole Chicken (6.5 lbs.)	360	75

Fish and Seafood	Temp (°F)	Time (min)
Calamari (8 oz.)	400	4
Fish Fillet (1-inch, 8 oz.)	400	10
Salmon Fillet (6 oz.)	380	12
Tuna Steak	400	7 to 10
Scallops	400	5 to 7
Shrimp	400	5

Frozen Foods	Temp (°F)	Time (min)
Onion Rings (12 oz.)	400	8
Thin French Fries (20 oz.)	400	14
Thick French Fries (17 oz.)	400	18
Pot Sticks (10 oz.)	400	8
Fish Sticks (10 oz.)	400	10
Fish Fillets (½-inch, 10 oz.)	400	14

Appendix 3 Recipes Index

A
Air Fried Cheese Sticks with Low-Carb Ketchup 22
Air Fried Marjoram Lamb Chops 40

B
Baked Salmon Steaks with Butter and Wine 49
Basic Vanilla Cupcakes 60
BBQ Chicken Wings 33

C
Cauliflower Egg Bake 23
Cheese Black and Blue Burgers 43
Cheese Broccoli Tots 51
Cheesy Broccoli Balls 22
Chocolate & Courgette Muffins 24
Chocolate Cookies 58
Creamy Broccoli Puree 52
Crispy Broccoli Tots 29
Crispy Cheese Mushroom Balls 20
Crispy Chicken Nuggets 34
Crispy Chicken Tenders 35
Crispy Chocolate Chips Cookies 62
Crispy Fish Fillets 47
Crispy Onion Rings with Mayo Dip 21
Crispy Red Beetroot Chips 53
Crispy Spinach-Cheese Balls 19

D
Delicious Beef Bulgogi Burgers 41
Delicious Chocolate Mascarpone Cake 64
Delicious Scrambled Egg Muffins 19
Dijon Chuck Eye Steak 44

E
Easy Aubergine Bites 52
Easy Gingered Chicken Drumsticks 33
Easy Popcorn Chicken Balls 58
Easy Roasted Asparagus 28

F
Fajita Meatball Lettuce Wraps 42
Flavourful Cheese Cauliflower Casserole 27
Flavourful Fluffy Chocolate Cake 59
Flavourful Greek Omelet with Cheese 20
Flavourful Tuna Patties 46
French Sea Bass with Sauce 48
Fresh Blackberry Muffins 63
Fried Potato Cubes 30
Fried Prawns Skewers 46

G
Garlic Lamb Chops 40

H
Healthy Broccoli Hash Brown 51
Healthy Roasted Turkey Breasts 36
Homemade Black Bean Arepas 25
Homemade Cheesy Mushroom Burgers 43
Homemade Double Chocolate Brownies 61
Honeyed Chicken Wings 54

L
Lamb Meatballs 41

P
Pork Patties with Blue Cheese 42

Q
Quick Brussels Sprouts 29
Quick Peppermint Lamb Chops 39
Quick Tortilla Chips 54

R
Refreshing Apple Vinegar Chicken Breast 37
Roasted Brussels Sprouts 53
Roasted Chicken Thighs 34
Roasted Dijon Asparagus 27
Roasted Kabocha Squash 28
Roasted Lemony Prawns 49
Roasted Spiced Lamb Cutlets 39
Roasted Thanksgiving Turkey Breast 35
Roasted Turkey Sausage with Cauliflower 36

S
Simple Bagels 24
Simple Cheese-Stuffed Mushrooms 55
Simple Cheesy Courgette Bake 31
Simple Salmon Patties 48
Simple Spanish Churros 62
Soft Blueberry Cupcakes 61
Spicy Juicy Chicken Drumsticks 55
Spicy Pickle Relish Deviled Eggs 21
Spicy Prawns and Cherry Tomato Kebabs 47
Sweet Espresso Brownies 60
Sweet-and-Spicy Spare Ribs 56

T
Tasty Cheese Veggie Quesadilla 30
Tasty Chocolate Lava Cake 63
Traditional Scotch Eggs 23

Y
Yummy Chocolate Brownies 59

Printed in Great Britain
by Amazon